GREATNESS *in* *Our* TEENAGERS

A 10 STEP GUIDE FOR PARENTS AND EDUCATORS

PETER TASSI AND FILOMENA TASSI

Paulist Press
New York/Mahwah, NJ

The Scripture quotations contained herein are from the New Revised Standard Version: Catholic Edition Copyright © 1989 and 1993, by the Division of Christian Education of the National Council of the Churches of Christ in the United States of America. Used by permission. All rights reserved.

"Slow Me Down, Lord," by Wilferd A. Peterson in his book *Adventures in the Art of Living*, Simon & Schuster, 1968, used with permission. All rights reserved.

"Please Hear What I'm Not Saying," by Charles C. Finn, used with permission of author, www.poetrybycharlescfinn.com. All rights reserved.

Cover design and book design by Lynn Else

Library of Congress Cataloging-in-Publication Data

Tassi, Peter.
    Greatness in our teenagers : a 10 step guide for parents and educators / Peter Tassi and Filomena Tassi.
        p. cm.
    ISBN 978-0-8091-4604-8 (alk. paper)
    1. Parent and teenager—Religious aspects—Christianity. 2. Parenting—Religious aspects—Christianity. 3. Child rearing—Religious aspects—Christianity. 4. Christian education of children. 5. Church work with teenagers. 6. Self-actualization (Psychology) in adolescence. I. Tassi, Filomena. II. Title.
    BV4529.T33 2009
    248.8'45—dc22

2009011666

Published by Paulist Press
997 Macarthur Boulevard
Mahwah, New Jersey 07430

www.paulistpress.com

Printed and bound in the
United States of America

CONTENTS

Foreword v

Preface: An Easy-to-Follow 10 Step Formula vii

Acknowledgments ix

1. Begin with Yourself 1

2. Nourish and Develop Their Faith 15

3. Help Them Find Meaning in Their Lives 21

4. Create Opportunities for Them 36

5. Challenge Them 43

6. Create a Sense of Belonging 52

7. Help Them Discover Their Talents and Passions....................60

8. Guide Them to Models and Mentors......................................68

9. Love and Respect Them Unconditionally 73

10. Give Them Enough Autonomy to Have Confidence..............80

Conclusion: Light and Hope...87

We dedicate this book to our late father, Phil Tassi,
and our mother, Irene Tassi. God has blessed us with
these beautiful and loving parents, who taught us the life
and message of Jesus through how they lived, loved, and cared
for all of God's creation. We are shaped by those we love
and, therefore, much of our work is a reflection
of our parents' beauty.

FOREWORD

Greatness in Our Teenagers is a most needed book, written with a great sense of respect for youth and their families. Blessed with deep insight into the challenge of raising youth today and with appreciation for their social, physical, and spiritual needs, Filomena and Peter Tassi have pulled together years of personal and pastoral experience.

Written clearly and beautifully, Filomena and Peter have tackled the most challenging vocation of working with and parenting youth. They address the need for mercy, hope, forgiveness, and patience in our daily struggles to understand and nurture teenagers. Making use of beautiful verses from scripture, personal stories, insights from influential persons, and their own heartfelt prayers, Filomena and Peter present us with practical and spiritual steps toward effective communication with youth.

Having worked with youth and being a mother of four children, ages four to twenty-one, I have found this book to be most helpful, practical, and spiritually uplifting. I relate to the many stories and examples, and I benefit from Filomena and Peter's experience. I have had the pleasure of working with both of these fine individuals as colleagues in campus ministry, and I am thrilled that they are sharing their gifts and insights with others.

Rooted in Christ's mercy, this book is sure to inspire and offer hope. I recommend it wholeheartedly to all parents, caregivers, youth workers, and educators, and to all others who share in Christ's ministry of feeding the hungry, giving shelter to the homeless, offering drink to the thirsty, and sharing God's love with the lonely and despairing.

Josephine Lombardi
Assistant Professor of Pastoral/Systematic Theology
St. Augustine's Seminary, Scarborough, Ontario

PREFACE

An Easy-to-Follow 10 Step Formula

Remember that you were without Christ,...having no hope and without God in the world. But now in Christ Jesus you who once were far off have been brought near through the blood of Christ.   (Eph 2:12–13)

Our goal in this book is to help you as parent or educator (including teacher, principal, vice-principal, educational assistant, chaplain, and social worker) to relate to, and bring out the best in, your children or students. Whether you are working with a child who is struggling desperately, or with a child who simply cannot seem to "find their way," this book was written to help you. We have created a *10 Step Formula* that may be applied to all youth. The formula is easy to understand and practical. The most challenging task required of you is that you adapt to a new way of "seeing" our youth and working with them. If you are able to do this, you will be able to unleash the greatness that is within them. Upon doing so, you will experience great joy and great satisfaction.

The book consists of ten chapters, each chapter revealing one step of the formula. Every chapter includes stories, personal experiences, and insights, as well as scripture quotes and prayers. At the end of each chapter, we conclude with *Practical Tips* and *Points to Ponder.* The Practical Tips serve as summary points, offering direction on how to be successful in applying the formula. The Points to Ponder help you to evaluate your own mindset and reflect on your own actions to insure you are on the right track. Finally, we provide *Spiritual Exercises*, which may be conducted in your home or in the classroom. These exercises will assist both you and your students or children to grow in faith, love, and understanding of each other. If you work through this book, we are confident that you will meet with success.

ACKNOWLEDGMENTS

We thank many who have served as our inspiration and guide over the years:

Fr. Lou Quinn (1928–2007), who demonstrated that each person is deserving of love, dignity, and respect

John Valvasori and Nat Gallo, who have shown the importance of leading with humility and prudence

Teachers and school staff, who have given of themselves wholly and completely in an effort to actualize each student's God-given gifts

Sharon Boase and Paul Bentley, who have offered continuous support, direction, and encouragement in a loving effort to insure this book made it onto the shelves

Thank you all.

Chapter One

BEGIN WITH YOURSELF

MODEL THE LOVE AND FORGIVENESS OF JESUS

> Be imitators of God, as beloved children, and live in love, as Christ loved us and gave himself up for us, a fragrant offering and sacrifice to God. (Eph 5:1–2)

Jesus approaches sinners and forgives them for their sins. In many cases he does this without them asking for forgiveness. His act of love is extended without any guarantee of their repentance or conversion. Jesus simply forgives. Perhaps in this powerful act of forgiveness, Jesus attempts to change their hearts and, consequently, their lives. This conversion of the lives he touched could not have occurred without these divine acts of mercy.

Jesus provides us with powerful, living witness in these actions. He encourages us to be generous with our love and to be willing to forgive without being asked. Jesus' ultimate act of love is revealed when he offers love and forgiveness to those who hurt him: "Father, forgive them, for they do not know what they are doing" (Luke 23:34). The Romans and the Jews who were involved in the plot to kill Jesus did not ask for forgiveness. In fact, they were convinced that their actions were righteous and just. They believed themselves more deserving of praise than of forgiveness. Yet, Jesus asks his father to forgive them, the people who crucified him.

We must attempt to emulate the mercy of Jesus and show our youth that we love them. We may not always feel that love. Some of us may have to search deep within ourselves to find it. However, the love is there. Once we find it, we must demonstrate to them that, no matter what happens, we will never give up on them and we will always be there for them. They must come to know, through our actions and words, that our love for them is powerful beyond measure and unfailing.

This does not mean that we advocate tolerating deviant or unacceptable behavior. It does not mean that we are not tough with our children or students and don't discipline them when necessary. However, if we can demonstrate to them a fraction of the love that Jesus revealed to us, then we will have successfully accomplished two things: First, we give them a glimpse of Jesus' divine mercy. This will make them feel worthy and deserving of love. It will enable them to accept their own frailty and continue to feel good about themselves despite their own failings. It will restore their dignity, for they will recognize themselves as children of God.

Second, it will empower them and fill them with confidence and ambition. It is our love that will enable them to overcome every obstacle. Demonstrating our love is not difficult. It begins with the simplest of acts. All youth, including the most troubled, are strongly influenced by simple acts of love. They can be delighted over a friendly greeting, a special interest in how their weekend went, or an offer to assist them with work they find difficult.

Conversely, they can be saddened by the simplest of gestures, such as not acknowledging their presence or not paying attention to them. You may not even be conscious of your actions. However, be mindful of everything you say and everything you do, because you are being watched and listened to intently. Never underestimate the impact of your words and gestures and make every effort to keep your actions positive and generous. When our youth know that we are there for them, that we walk the journey with them, that we believe there is greatness within them, their own sense of hope comes alive.

Accepting our teenagers in all their frailty and sinfulness can be difficult, particularly when we have suffered the consequences of their erroneous ways. However, it is essential for success. It is in our act of forgiveness, and our willingness to love them unconditionally, that we can change their hearts. It demonstrates to them that nothing is greater than our love for them. When they realize we stood by them, even when they were in error, our actions become truly healing.

The following story demonstrates the kind of mercy that our youth possess. They have a great capacity to forgive despite the fact that they are in a world that has often been unforgiving.

Brenda was in tears when she first came to my office. Unlike many troubled teens, Brenda exuded a powerful physical strength. However, her body language and her eyes told me that she was weak and broken. It was our first meeting. She was sixteen.

As soon as she sat in the chair across from me, she began to sob. She began to explain that she was born in Poland. Her mother had left her father for another man when she was five years old. Her mother took Brenda with her to live with this new man. Her father left the country to begin a new life somewhere else.

The new man in her mother's life would not accept Brenda. To him, Brenda was nothing but a burden. Brenda's mother had to make a choice between her daughter and her boyfriend. She chose her boyfriend. She sent Brenda to live with her grandparents in Canada.

For ten years, Brenda mourned the loss of her mother. Finally, her mother left the boyfriend and came to Canada to be with Brenda. Brenda was ecstatic. She immediately forgave her mother and felt whole and happy. Within eight months, Brenda's mother met another man. He too would not accept Brenda, and again her mother sent her to live with her grandparents and left the city to be with this new man.

"My mother has chosen a man over me," she sobbed. "Twice my mother has left me for someone else."

Feeling heartbroken and helpless, I searched for the proper words to bring her comfort. I simply said, "Brenda, I'm sorry. I hope you know that you are okay and it is your mother who is not okay." I did not know if Brenda felt any better after leaving my office, but I certainly didn't. Brenda left, and I cried.

Although Brenda and I saw each other a couple more times before the end of the year, I didn't know what advice to give her or what I could do to make her situation any better. All I could do was listen and reassure her that she was a beautiful child worthy of infinite love, and that there was nothing wrong with her.

We returned to school in September. It was October when I saw Brenda again, roughly six months after her mother had left her for the second time. I asked her if she had seen her mother. She said that she had not, but they spoke occasionally on the phone.

"And how are you doing?" I asked.

"I have come to accept it, sir," she replied.

"How did you arrive at that point?" I asked.

"I understand that my mother loves me, but her problem is that she loves herself more. That's just the way she is and she can't help it."

I looked at Brenda with a puzzled and worried expression. I worried that she may have been saying this just so that I wouldn't worry about her.

I couldn't understand her great capacity to forgive. Brenda noticed my expression and quickly added:

"Don't worry, sir, I know that I'm okay and my mother is not. I have forgiven her for the way she is."

_____

At this moment the face of Jesus was revealed in this young girl. It was a beauty that is beyond words.

BE STRONG IN YOUR FAITH

> "I will show you what someone is like who comes to me, hears my words, and acts on them. That one is like a man building a house, who dug deeply and laid the foundation on rock; when a flood arose, the river burst against that house but could not shake it, because it had been well built."   (Luke 6:47–48)

It is critical that we keep a strong spiritual base and remain rooted in Christ throughout this journey. This provides us with strength, commitment, and insight. Remember that on this journey we are only mediators, instruments doing God's great work. To survive, we must trust in God and recognize God's grace at work in our lives and in the lives of the children we live with and/or work with. God is calling us and calling them. We listen to Jesus' words in Matthew 16:24, where he says: "If any want to become my followers, let them deny themselves and take up their cross and follow me."

No matter what role we have in the lives of youth, we must see our work as a vocation. We are called to inspire and be inspired. There will be situations like Brenda's where we can't say or do much to make a difference. We can't take away their pain, suffering, or struggle. However, God calls us to this ministry as parent, principal, teacher, educational assistant, chaplain, social worker, or friend. We are instruments of God's love and God's healing power. Remain rooted in faith and be confident that, in all you do, God as Father, Son, and Holy Spirit is present and God's grace is with you.

SEE STRENGTH IN WEAKNESS

> [The Lord] said to me, "My grace is sufficient for you, for power is made perfect in weakness." So I will boast all the more gladly

4

of my weaknesses, so that the power of Christ may dwell in me.

(2 Cor 12:9)

We reflect on the teachings of Jesus, as expressed by St. Paul in 2 Corinthians 11:30, illustrating that in weakness, there is strength; in failure, victory; and in the cross, resurrection. Paul says, "If I must boast, I will boast of the things that show my weakness." It is often a difficult task to see strength in weakness. However, weakness is often the cause of a person's strength or special talent.

Consider the "Story of the Diamond" that I recall one of my professors used in a theology class over thirty years ago to illustrate this point.

There was a king who possessed the largest and most beautiful diamond in the world. It was so large and beautiful that it was priceless. However, the diamond had a flaw. At the top of the diamond was a chip that had an irregular shape, spreading slightly outward. It troubled the king greatly that this priceless diamond had been flawed. He summoned craftsmen from all over his kingdom to repair the diamond and rid it of this flaw. Many suggestions were offered: sand out the flaw until it could no longer be seen; chip out more of the diamond around the flaw to create a smooth surface; break the diamond into many beautiful small diamonds and discard the flawed part. The king was not happy with any of these suggestions.

The king issued a second edict. He would give half his kingdom and his daughter in marriage to anyone who could fix the diamond. This offer brought craftsmen from many nations. None of them could find a satisfactory solution.

Finally, some nobles who believed that this man's wisdom might result in an answer pleasing to the king brought a poor peasant to the king. The peasant took the diamond and held it in his hand. After studying the flaw, he reached down and took from the ground a sharp rock. He then pressed the sharp point of the stone against the flaw in the diamond and carved into the diamond a long winding line leading down from the flaw to the bottom of the diamond.

The king screamed, "What are you doing? You fool, you ruined my diamond."

The peasant handed the diamond to the king and said to him: "Look."

The king studied the diamond and what he thought destroyed this priceless stone actually enhanced its beauty. This diamond now had carved in it the most beautiful long stemmed rose.

This story is about finding strength in weakness. Let us attempt to adopt a new attitude toward weaknesses. Teenage weaknesses may not only lead us to their strengths, but their weaknesses may in fact be the home of their *greatest* strengths. It is in their weaknesses that we may discover in them beautiful and wondrous gifts. The question that arises for us adults is, "Are we willing to embrace their weakness and, in doing this, discover their gift?"

The next story about Joshua is another helpful example about this point.

When Joshua was born, he weighed just over one pound. The doctors said he would not survive, and if he did, he would be a dwarf, would be physically handicapped, and would live with severe brain damage. Joshua did survive and, with the aid of growth hormones and a lot of love from his family, he grew to be a loving, intelligent, and gentle young man. At the same time, he lived with many physical hardships.

He remained, although not a dwarf, no taller than four feet. His legs were disfigured and he found walking difficult. His hands and fingers were twisted, which made it difficult for him to write and perform many "normal" tasks. His body was crooked, his head and face disfigured. In spite of all of this, it never took away his love for life and his desire to try everything. He had a wonderful appreciation for the smallest of things.

One day Joshua came into my office and asked me, "Sir, do you think there actually is a heaven?"

I paused as many thoughts raced through my mind. Then I wondered whether Joshua was going through a difficult time and was pondering on a better world.

"Yes!" I responded. "Of course there is a heaven."

"What do you think it's like in heaven?" Joshua quickly asked.

"Oh, it is beautiful, full of peace, health, and love," I replied.

To my surprise he asked, "You don't think it's better than here? Do you, sir?"

"What do you mean, not better than here?" I asked.

"Life is beautiful here, sir. We have everything and we can do anything. I have often wondered, that if there is a heaven, how can heaven be better than earth? And if it can't be better than earth, why would God create heaven?"

After Joshua left my office, I reflected, and I concluded that this young, physically deformed boy had found beauty. He had discovered beauty in spite of his weakness and perhaps within the very core of his weakness. He was blinded by the beauty of life.

When we approach teenagers and work with them, no matter what the state of their past or their present brokenness, in order for us to make any progress, we too must embrace them in all their weakness, and then we too will be blinded, blinded by the beauty within them.

This section concludes with a story heard during a homily at church that we hope provides you with a new way of seeing weakness:

There was once a famous concert pianist. He was coming to play in a local auditorium, and a mother wanted to take her little boy. Her son had been playing the piano for one year and she thought it would be wonderful for her child to see this master play. She went to the concert hall with her son and they were taking their seats. She heard a friend call her name. The mother crossed the aisle to say hello. They chatted momentarily, and then the lights began to dim. She turned to take her seat and noticed that her son was gone. She panicked and did not know what to do. Just then, the curtains opened and the spot light went on the piano. Seated at the piano was her son. She was overwhelmed by a sense of dread.

The boy began to play "Twinkle Twinkle Little Star." As he played, the master walked out onto the stage. He walked over to the piano and sat beside the boy. He whispered in the boy's ear, "Keep playing." The boy carried on and the master began to accompany him. The master was able to make the simple song sound truly wonderful. They finished and the audience broke into a thunderous applause. The master and boy both bowed. The master had transformed a potentially embarrassing situation into an inspiring performance.

COMMUNICATE WITH KINDNESS

> I would rather speak five words with my mind, in order to instruct others also, than ten thousand words in a tongue.
>
> (1 Cor 14:19)

Communication is the foundation of a strong and healthy home. It is a necessary ingredient for developing a good relationship with our children and with our students. Without good communication, it is almost impossible to make progress with youth. They desire communication. Communication takes many forms: thought, speech, and action.

To build strong lines of communication we must *say* the right things, *do* the right things, and *think* the right things.

First, by *saying* the right things, we as parents should make use of two very powerful statements and make use of them as often as possible. These are, "I love you" and "I am proud of you." Don't be fooled when your children squint or squirm when they hear these words. They may pretend to be embarrassed; they are not. They love to hear these words. In fact, they long to hear them. These words have a very powerful impact. As educators, the phrases we chose will vary, depending on our relationship and comfort level with each student. Even simple phrases—like "How are you doing today?" or "May I help you with your school work?"—will go a long way in demonstrating our care and concern for our students.

Second, we must *do* the right things. When doing the right things, our actions should be pure and our motives genuine. If love, kindness, and gentleness are at the root of all our actions, our youth will be calmed and want to emulate us. Further, as parents, we must offer our youth lots of physical contact. This means lots of hugs and kisses. Again, they may seem to shy away from this; however, they actually crave this kind of affection. They need it. It affirms them. Physical contact is a strong expression of affirmation and the love we have for them.

It is unfortunate that we have developed a "hands off" policy when it comes to kids who are not our own children. As understandable as it is, given the sexual abuse so many children have suffered, it is still sad. Touch is a powerful, comforting, and healing form of communication. We all need to be touched, hugged, and shown healthy physical affection. Jesus constantly used touch to affirm and to heal.

The following story demonstrates the importance of touch.

While working in the House of Malnutrition with the Sisters of Charity in Haiti, I discovered many wonderful treasures. Row upon row there were children suffering from terrible and deplorable diseases, from AIDS to malnutrition. They cried with their suffering.

However, I experienced that when I held them, they stopped crying. Feeding them, changing them, and medicating them did not always stop their cries. As soon as they were picked up, the crying turned to a whimper. As I held them close to my chest and rocked them, their whimpers turned to silence. They would then fall asleep in my arms. All they wanted, in all their suffering, was to be touched and held.

It is important to spend quality time and *quantity* time with youth. Don't be misled by the quality time theory. For our youth, quantity is every bit as important as quality. Many parents have told us that their teenagers are independent and don't need them around. For example, parents report that even when they are home with their kids, there is not much being said. Their kids are in their rooms, watching television or on the computer. Yet, they are mistaken to conclude that they need not be home for their kids. Our children want us at home, whether we are communicating with them or not. They want to know that we are there and that they can turn to us at anytime. They find security and comfort knowing that we are present for them.

Further, there will be brief moments when some event occurs and they wish to communicate with us. If we are home, this connection will happen. If we are not home, it is a missed opportunity for us and our children. This does not mean we need to live imprisoned in our homes; however, time at home with our teenagers is well-invested time. Our presence reassures them that we are concerned about them. They notice when we choose to be at home with them rather than out at meetings, dinner parties, or social events. Lots of physical affection, combined with quantity and quality time, will help build strong lines of communication.

Third, we must *think* the right things. Our thoughts must be pure. Our children and maybe our students can "read" our thoughts. What we "do not say," as well as our body language, speaks louder than the spoken word. All that we do, think, and say must be pure and genuine. We must abandon our notions that teenagers are selfish, vulgar, angry, hostile, or lazy. They are not. Show us a teenager that possesses any of these traits, and for each one, we will show you hundreds that do not. Do not succumb to these stereotypes; they are erroneous, unhealthy, and destructive. We must strive to know in our minds and hearts the great potential in our teenagers and to believe we can assist in actualizing that potential. When we believe this, our teenagers will be empowered through our confidence in them.

Building healthy lines of communication and a strong relationship with your child or student is not complicated but it does involve sacrifice and humility. Here are "Ten Commandments of Communication," based on what teenagers have shared with us over the years.

Ten Commandments for Communicating with Youth

1. *Listen to Them*
   Don't interrupt. Reserve your comments and give advice only when you are asked.

2. *Remain Open-Minded*
   Don't assume or prejudge; put yourself in their world.

3. *Trust in Them*
   Give them autonomy to hold their own views.

4. *Understand Them*
   Don't complain about what they say, even when it may hurt
   you or run contrary to your views. Let them know that it is
   important to you that you understand them.

5. *Respect Them*
   Respect their words and actions, their choices and judgments.

6. *Be a Friend*
   Talk to them about their day, their problems, and their interests.

7. *Show Support*
   Talk about and show interest in the things they are interested
   in. Give them the support they need to move forward with
   conviction and confidence.

8. *Be Honest*
   Don't assume that you know all the answers or that you are
   always right. Share your thoughts and stories honestly.

9. *Be Patient*
   Watch TV, eat meals, and shop with them, giving them quality
   and quantity time.

10. *Accept Them*
    Don't try to make them someone you want them to be. Accept
    them as they are.

These "commandments" may sometimes seem difficult to follow, but
it is our experience that they will lead to a much greater understanding
and closer relationship with your teens.

LOOK FOR THE MOMENT

We have not ceased praying for you and asking that you may
be filled with knowledge of God's will in all spiritual wisdom
and understanding, so that you may lead lives worthy of the

Lord, fully pleasing to him, as you bear fruit in every good work and as you grow in the knowledge of God.   (Col 1:9–10)

Perhaps the most important point to remember in this chapter is to look for that "moment," that "flash of light." As you are making your way through these steps, you will witness a moment where you have connected. This connection, or light, will show itself in one of many ways: a word they speak, a look in their eye, a change in their posture, a moment of deeper interest. There will be a sign, perhaps very subtle, but once identified, you will have found an opportunity. It may be discovered while discussing issues and topics completely independent of what troubles them. However, while they talk, you will see it. Once you discover it, seize it, explore it, and focus on it.

REMAIN HOPE-FILLED

Our hope for you is unshaken; for we know that as you share in our sufferings, so also you share in our consolation. (2 Cor 1:7)

Never give up hope! Be extremely patient, devoting much of your time and energy to working with your children or students. When you become frustrated and exhausted, be sure to take a break, but never give up. Always believe that any obstacle can be overcome. We know that buried deep within our youth is the potential for greatness. God created each of them in God's likeness, with infinite beauty, wisdom, and love. God will give you the strength, courage, patience, and the wisdom you will need to mend the brokenness and discover the greatness. God has entrusted this child to you. As difficult as it may be, God calls you to be a forgiving voice, loving heart, and guiding light. Don't give up hope.

Take comfort in knowing that in hope there comes strength, and in strength great joy. For even in the midst of the struggle and suffering, we are doing what God is calling us to do.

I remember asking one of the sisters in the House of Malnutrition, "Sister, would you like to come back to Canada with me? It is beautiful in Canada and there are no such sights as these. You will have a nice home, health care, opportunity, food, and cleanliness."

She quickly replied, "No thank you." I continued by asking, "Why do you choose this life over the life Canada offers?"

She answered, "Because God called me to this life." I quickly responded, "But this life is cruel and hard and full of suffering and sadness."

She smiled and said, "When you do what God calls you to do, you receive great joy even when you are in such suffering and sadness."

We, as parents and educators, have been called by God to do what is difficult. But, we will receive joy and reward in the midst of our sacrifice for doing what God calls us to do.

In order to be successful in working with teens, we must first examine our own way of thinking, living, and working. As difficult as it may be to transform ourselves, we know that in this process our suffering will be well served. It will make us more effective in our work and our lives will be enriched. We will see our work as more than just "making a living." It will become natural for us to do what we can to make a difference in the children we work with and in the world itself.

As we embark on this journey, we know that we are not alone!

"Footprints in the Sand." Author Anonymous

One night a man had a dream. He dreamed he was walking along
the beach with the Lord.
Across the sky flashed scenes from his life.
For each scene he noticed two sets of footprints in the sand:
one belonging to him, and the other to the Lord.
When the last scene of his life flashed before him,
he looked back at the footprints in the sand.
He noticed that many times along the path of his life,
there was only one set of footprints.
He also noticed that it happened at the very lowest and saddest
times in his life.
This really bothered him and he questioned the Lord about it:
"Lord, you said that once I decided to follow you, you'd walk with
me all the way.
But I have noticed that during the most troublesome times in my
life, there is only one set of footprints.
I don't understand why, when I needed you most, that you would
leave me."

The Lord replied:

"My son, my precious child, I love you and I would never leave you.
During your times of trial and suffering, when you see only one set
  of footprints,
it was then that I carried you."

PRACTICAL TIPS

- Let go and let God!
- Pause…take time to replenish yourself spiritually.
- Stop and think before acting or reacting: What would Jesus do?
- Remember that you are not the Messiah; you are his
  humble and faithful servant.
- Reflect on this quotation by a priest: "I am only a hungry
  beggar telling other hungry beggars where I get my food."

POINTS TO PONDER

- Do I find it difficult to express my love, care, and concern
  for my children or students? When is the last time I said,
  "I love you," or "I care about you?" (as parent), or "How is
  your day going?" (as educator).
- When you look deep into your child's or a student's eyes,
  what do you see?
- Are you feeling you are going to be successful in reaching
  your child or student? Why? Why not?

SPIRITUAL EXERCISES

EXERCISE ONE

1. Begin by finding a quiet place and pray the following:

"Slow Me Down, Lord"

Slow me down, Lord. Give me, amid the confusion of the day,
the calmness of the everlasting hills. Break the tensions of my

nerves and muscles with the soothing music of the singing streams that live in my memory. Help me to know the magical, restoring power of relaxation. Teach me the art of taking minute vacations of slowing down to look at a flower, to chat with a friend, to pat a dog, to read a few lines from a good book. Remind me each day of the fable of the hare and the tortoise, that I may know that the race is not always to the swift. There is more to life than increasing its speed. Let me look upward into the branches of the towering oak and know that it grew great and strong because it grew slowly and well. Slow me down, Lord, and inspire me to send my roots deep into the soil of life's enduring values that I may grow toward the stars of my greater destiny.

Amen.

2. Pray to Jesus, asking him to help you and be near to you.

Look at the image below, focusing on the four black dots in the center for thirty seconds, and then gently close your eyes. Speak from your heart to the person who appears to you.

Chapter Two

NOURISH AND DEVELOP
THEIR FAITH

> "Truly, I tell you that unless you change and become like children, you will never enter the kingdom of heaven." (Matt 18:3)

We teach youth about God yet many youth already "know God." We can teach church history, sacramental theology, and scripture, but many youth already think, breathe, and live the gospel.

> At that time the disciples came to Jesus and asked, "Who is the greatest in the kingdom of heaven?" He called a child, whom he put among them, and said, "Truly I tell you, unless you change and become like children, you will never enter the kingdom of heaven. Whoever becomes humble like this child is the greatest in the kingdom of heaven. Whoever welcomes one such child in my name welcomes me." (Matt 18:1–5)

When we read this passage, we see that Jesus must have envisioned the kingdom of God when he looked at the faith of children. We ask ourselves: "What is it that Jesus saw?" The people of his day certainly did not see it; they tried to prevent the children from seeing Jesus. They viewed children as unworthy and without status.

In education it is our function to give students as much knowledge and theology as possible. We cannot underestimate the importance of the study of religion and scriptures. This knowledge will help our youth to better know and understand Jesus. *However*, it is a mistake to view our role as solely imparting knowledge, whether we are educators, parents, or role models. Deepening youth's relationship with Jesus goes beyond the transmission of knowledge.

Many children already have a good basis for faith development. It was given at birth and has been nurtured in their learning and their experiences from infancy through to adolescence. It is important to recognize that there is a difference between being religious and being spiritual. Children and teens are spiritual but sometimes not religious. They show great potential in their acts of kindness, their innate generosity toward the poor, their support for each other, their deep sensitivity, and their purity and innocence of heart. Their compassion and acts are an embodiment of their spirituality. It is our mission to root this spirituality in Jesus our Savior.

Faith development and spiritual growth are easy to foster in our young people. It is through our own acts of love, kindness, understanding, patience, consideration, and encouragement that we teach these children about Jesus. They will ask themselves why adults act this way, why they reach out this way, why they sacrifice to make the lives of others better. Our young people will then come to understand that the answer resides in our faith, in our humanity, in who we truly are. They will identify that each of us lives this way because it is what we "truly are" as a human being. In turn, this cultivates their already-existing desire to be one with their own true nature, their Christ-nature.

They will be comforted to see that faith demands more than following commandments. Faith is a way of living, loving, and caring. Our living witness will have a profound impact on our youth because, instinctively and naturally, they truly are people of faith with the desire at the core of their being to be one with the divine nature of Christ. Our teens are already filled with Christ. There resides deep within them infinite beauty, wisdom, and love. We may look at some of our youth and have trouble seeing them as faith-filled. Many rebel and move away from the institutional aspect of religion, particularly when it is presented in an aggressive way. They do not want more rules. They do not want to be told what to do or how to worship. However, they possess great faith. Their spirituality runs deep and we must approach them in a new way, challenging them to become leaders of our community and our church. We can do this in two ways.

First, we must think of creative ways to make their spirituality, faith, and church come alive for them. In our own experience, trips to the Third World are profoundly transforming. However, this opportunity is not always available to everyone, so we suggest working locally for the needy.

It makes youth feel they are making a meaningful contribution. Also, it fulfils the love and beauty that already reside within them. They begin to ask deeper questions and to seek answers. This is a great opportunity for them to come in touch with their Christ-nature.

Second, we must demonstrate how much the church needs them and invite them to become active members in their own church. They will accept the institutional aspect of their religion and welcome it with open arms when we can speak their language and make them feel welcomed and needed. They will accept the institutional church when they recognize it as a model of service rather than a model of rules. They will embrace the institutional church when they believe that their voice is heard, their opinions are respected, and their contributions are valued.

We must recognize that their input and involvement are critical and must bring young people to this same understanding. Who needs whom? Do our young people need the church or does the church need our young people? When young people reject religion, it needs to be pointed out to them that they are spiritual people and that their spirituality is an inspiration to us. Like Jesus, we must push away the crowd of naysayers and insist that our children come forward. We have to give them the assurance that they are a faith-filled people who can inspire us. Their innocent, childlike faith reflects the kingdom of God. It is our responsibility as parents and educators to cultivate this spirituality that already exists, confirming what they already believe: that their true nature is the Christ-nature. We are the facilitators for God.

The most spiritual and compassionate kids we have met were raised by parents who rarely quoted from scripture and did not constantly remind their children of the commandments. They *lived* the scriptures, and that was far more important. They modeled the way of Jesus in how they treated others, and how they were caring, considerate, compassionate, generous, and thoughtful people. Their children became faith-filled through example and living witness in all that their parents said, did, and thought.

We can give many examples of the evidence of this deep spirituality that exists within our youth. One such example is their willingness to reach out to those in need. When they are asked to bring clothes for the homeless, they will deliver a truckload. When they are called upon to go out and feed the hungry, they will fill a bus. When they are asked to raise money for the poor, they will raise thousands.

One of our youth gave generously and quietly of his time as this following story illustrates.

The president of the student council dropped by my office. He asked me about an upcoming event that we were working on together. He was yawning and looked quite tired. This seemed out of character for him since he was always full of energy and highly motivated. I asked him if his schoolwork was keeping him up late.

"No, Miss, I got up pretty early this morning."

"How early?" I asked. He answered, "5:00 a.m."

I couldn't imagine why he needed to get up so early. I asked, "Why so early?"

He answered, "I adopted a child in the Third World and to support that child I took on a morning paper route. The money I earn I send to the child."

I was deeply touched. He passed it off as "no big deal." He said he would look at the child's picture on his fridge every morning and that gave him the energy to deliver the papers. I had worked with this student for four years and this was the first I had heard of this great sacrifice he had made to help someone so far away who was in great need. He took on this initiative on his own and was very happy about doing it, in his own quiet and humble way.

Another example that assures us of the great spirituality of our youth is their behavior at religious services and the respect they give religious leaders. During our school prayer services, we gather as many as 1,800 students in a gymnasium. During these services, you can hear a pin drop. Some of the schools in which we have worked are inner-city schools where many students take drugs or steal cars on the weekends. Some are promiscuous and earn their living on the street. However, when clergy and pastoral ministers visit the school, the language in the halls and the volume of chaos and noise quickly change. This change is not out of fear, as many of these kids know no fear. Their response is a reflection of their deep spirituality and their respect for spiritual leaders. These leaders represent to youth the goodness and wholesomeness of life. The behavior of the students reflects what is deep within them and wants to get out. The gymnasium becomes a "holy place" where they can go to rest their heads and hearts, find solace and peace, and perhaps turn away from this world for a little while and speak with God who understands them.

Keep looking for the deep spirituality that is within them. They may not describe themselves as religious or faith-filled, yet they are. I recall going into a religion class where the teacher asked, "On a scale of one to ten, how would each of you rate yourself in terms of how religious you are?" A couple of students answered six or seven; however, the majority ranked themselves under five. After a full discussion of "what it means to be religious," most realized that they were really a nine or ten.

Our goal ultimately is to root their spirituality in Jesus. This is actually an easy task. Our youth relate to Jesus. They love Jesus, who worked for justice; showed endless mercy, love, and understanding; who associated with sinners, defended the poor, and fought for the weak and downtrodden. Teenagers love to love, and they love to emulate the way of Jesus. It comes naturally to them. The rules, regulations, dogmas, and doctrines are secondary to them. They become interested in these topics only when they acknowledge that their church, their society, and their Jesus was concerned with *love*, and this love is expressed in acts of service and charity.

In concluding with this second step, always assume that within the child there is a great spirituality and a Christ-like nature. We do not have to impart it to them, but rather, we need to draw it out of them. We need to challenge them to lead, inspire, and show us the way. This approach breathes confidence and a new direction in our teens.

> Dear God:
> You have given each child a deep spirituality at birth.
> They have this great capacity to live an enlightened life,
> a life of faith, hope, and charity.
> Give us the tools we need to help your children unveil
> this great gift that lies deep within.
> Then, Lord, we ask you to give them
> the courage to live out this faith
> so that they, in their own way, can transform the world.
> Amen.

PRACTICAL TIPS

- Look for God in every child—God is there!
- Do not let a child's or student's reluctance to define themselves as religious make you believe they are not religious; children *are* faith-filled.
- Invite youth to *be* church—they have a great deal to offer.

· Rooting faith in Jesus is easy—he is already their hero and their friend.

POINTS TO PONDER

· Do you see God in your children or students?
· Why is Jesus so appealing to our youth? What traits do they find most endearing?
· What can you do to have our students or children know Jesus more intimately?

SPIRITUAL EXERCISES

EXERCISE ONE

1. Tell stories of inspiring heroes that sacrificed their lives for others. These may be heroes in your own community or stories you have heard from other states or countries. Such stories may include the mother who fought a cougar to protect her kids; the father who jumped in the water, although he could not swim, to save his child who was drowning; the passerby who goes into the house that is in flames to save people inside; the teen who hit a bear over the head with a branch to draw the bear away from his friend, who was being attacked.
2. Ask your students or children: "What makes a person put his or her life at risk?" and "Why do people do things that do not seem logical in order to save others?" Discuss the answers.
3. Ask the students or children to write a one- or two-page response to this question: "What are *you* willing to die for?"
4. Upon completion of these spiritual exercises, read John 15:13: "No one has greater love than this, to lay down one's life for one's friends." Discuss their interpretation of this gospel text.

Chapter Three

HELP THEM FIND MEANING IN THEIR LIVES

Now there are varieties of gifts, but the same Spirit; and there are varieties of services, but the same Lord; and there are varieties of activities, but it is the same God who activates all of them in everyone. To each is given the manifestation of the Spirit for the common good. (1 Cor 12:4–7)

REACHING OUTSIDE OF ONESELF

There are a high number of suicide attempts among our youth. When a teenager talks about suicide or when he or she actually attempts suicide, it is a cry for help. It is our experience that most teenagers do not want to take their own life; they are crying out to us, wanting to escape their suffering. They plan an attempt that will fail, and hope deep down that we will give them the attention and therapy that they require. Unfortunately, sometimes these suicide attempts are successful.

It is absolutely critical that teenagers who are depressed for long periods of time or who have fallen into a deep depression get medical attention. Medical doctors, psychologists, and psychiatrists can save a child by giving a proper diagnosis and prescribing proper medication and therapy. If you are unable to get help through your healthcare program, you must spend the time and the money to insure your child receives the help he or she needs. If you do not have the financial resources, you may wish to inquire with student services or the guidance department in the school (sometimes they can assist or offer direction).

Many youth experience darkness and depression because they see no meaning in their lives. They have lost their enthusiasm to live because there is nothing worth living for. This lack of purpose is the cause of enormous anxiety and a painful emptiness. Victor Frankl wrote a book describing the importance of having meaning in one's life, *Man's Search for Meaning*. In his book, Frankl points out the devastating effects of a life without meaning. For teenagers, this can lead to drugs (addictions), crime (aggression), and suicide. Our young people become lost because their lives have become meaningless. Their inability to understand the reason for living can lead to resentments, bitterness, a negative attitude, and anger, ultimately leading to destructive actions against themselves.

Despite their feelings of desperation and darkness, it is important that they *believe* there is a light. This is our task, to help them see this light. We need to assure them that although their feelings are all-consuming, they do not represent a permanent state. One day—whether with age, counseling, medication, or all three—these feelings of despair and loneliness will disappear. Depression can be temporary. There *is* a light, and small as it may appear, it shines at the top of that deep hole in which they find themselves. They need to climb a couple of rungs to see the flicker of light. We can help them by carrying them on our shoulders up those few rungs. Once they see that flicker of light, they will begin to slowly believe that there is hope.

There are different forms of suicide among our youth. For some, it is a quick and violent death through hanging, shooting, overdosing, or severing critical arteries. But for most, it is a slower method involving cutting themselves, drinking to excess, taking illegal drugs, joining gangs, or committing crimes. Although there are many other reasons for participating in such activities, youth know subconsciously that such participation can, and probably will, lead to their death.

These very kids often possess wonderful qualities such as kindness, gentleness, and compassion. Their suicidal behavior actually exemplifies a sense of false self, the opposite of what is truly within. For some it represents a total change in character. When they become melancholic and depressed, they are almost unrecognizable. They begin to ask themselves deeper questions and to feel isolation and loneliness at a much more intense level. They draw further and further away from us. We cannot help but ask ourselves: "How it is possible that this beautiful, gentle, sensitive kid can be involved in such a violent act toward her- or himself?"

It is difficult to understand fully why they have no desire to live and why they believe they have no reason for living, particularly in a society where there is such opportunity and prosperity for them. It is also difficult to understand their feelings of emptiness, loneliness, desperation, and depth of pain. It may be difficult to understand and it may not make sense, but it is very real.

Many teens travel this long road of destruction, awaiting some messiah to come along to rescue them. They will not express this but, in fact, it is their deep desire. However, we must not be surprised by their reaction when we step in to help. Youth will often not respond or will make an effort to distance themselves from us. Do not be discouraged. This is not because they do not want help. It may be because they do not believe we can help or they may feel ashamed and too proud to admit that help is required. Many are fearful and convinced we will not understand. However, our efforts must continue.

The question becomes, "What do we do to help them?" We can begin by speaking with them about *our* reasons for living, the things that fuel our energy, "causes" in the world that require our services. Then we focus on *them* and talk to them about causes that are in need of their attention and gifts. They have a responsibility to use the gifts they were given, and in the circumstances they face. Most importantly, the world needs what they have to offer. They have to realize that, in living out this purpose, in responding to this need, they will find meaning in their lives, for their actions will have the direct result of making the world a better place.

In this conversation, we are attempting to turn their attention to something outside of themselves. We want to direct them to something they value that is greater than they are. It can be a goal to achieve, a person to love, a talent to develop, a sensitivity to share, a mission to accomplish— all of which will be seen by them as causes beyond themselves that are greater than they are. We want them to see that there *is* meaning in their life, a reason and purpose to their existence. When they are able to reach outside of themselves and fulfill a purpose or respond to a need, their lives will gain greater significance and they will eventually find meaning. For each teenager, this meaning in life will be different, as each one of them is unique. They have different gifts, different talents, and different views of the world.

They also need to know that there is a strong network of people who care for and love them. They desire love desperately, and they need us to remind them that we do love them and that God loves them. No matter how useless and unlovable they feel, they must be constantly assured of the love we have for them and the love God has for them.

The following story shows children's need to be loved:

Valerie entered my office dejected and depressed. She was one of the many kids at our school who lived on the streets. Her mother did not have the patience to care for her and her father had a restraining order against him. Because of previous sexual assaults that she experienced at the hands of her father, he had been legally warned not to make any contact with her. I couldn't help but notice the scars on her wrist.

After a long discussion she revealed to me that she still saw her father, meeting him in his truck in secret places after school. She went on to explain how she would satisfy him sexually.

When I asked her why she would continue to allow herself to be abused and treated this way, she replied, "I need his love."

I took her hand and held it for a moment. All I could think of saying was, "You do not need your father's love. You have a father in heaven who loves you."

She cried and cried.

THE IMPORTANCE OF TEACHING VALUES

One of the most important roles that we have as parents and educators is to teach our youth about values. The gospels provide a great resource for determining the values we need to embrace in our daily lives. We look at the life of Jesus to find values that are important and worth nurturing. As our youth live their lives embracing gospel values, they will come to recognize their infinite worth.

Our job here is not an easy one because the values that our present North American culture supports are often contrary to gospel values. We need to reeducate and refocus our youth in the direction of gospel values. There are many examples to illustrate this point. A common one is in the area of materialism. Many of the students that we have counseled have come from affluent families. They have the opportunity for education, career, designer clothes, new cars, and many other luxuries. They are bombarded with messages that indicate that materialism is the key to happiness. They live in a world that tells them "Money brings happiness," "More is better," and "There is no such thing as too much." It's clear that accumulation of material possessions does not lead to happiness. Many people have material possessions and are lost, unhappy, and confused.

We share the following experience of one of our students. She did not find meaning or happiness in the place her parents thought she would.

It was early on a Sunday morning when I heard frantic knocking on my door at home. It was the parents of one of my students, desperate because their daughter had run away from home. I spent a couple of hours making phone calls before I finally found Tracy. I picked her up and brought her to my house.

This young girl had never been a problem in school, was an honor-roll student with a 90 percent average and had a wonderful personality and an angelic disposition. She had run away from home for a number of reasons: unreasonably high personal and academic expectations, physical forms of discipline, and a total lack of freedom and autonomy. Her parents were so strict and controlling that they were taking this gifted, bright, energetic child and destroying her.

At the same time, Tracy was aware that everything her parents did for her was done out of love. Although a twisted concept of love, it was love nevertheless. Tracy loved her parents. She believed, in fact, that the love between her and her parents was a powerful and almost profound love, but at the same time twisted, dysfunctional, and destructive.

Tracy stayed with my family over the next week. While she stayed with me, I enlisted another counselor who began the negotiation process between Tracy and her parents. This process took over a week before they could come to some civil terms and a temporary contract written for the purpose of getting Tracy back in the home.

Over that week I visited the parents a number of times. They lived in a luxurious, four-thousand square foot home. It boasted European leather furniture, including the finest of oak and mahogany. Every square foot of the house had the finest of flooring, carpeting, and decor. Tracy was now in my house, which was a modest bungalow. In fact, it was a handyman special. It was one-thousand square feet, with very little furniture, and no decor to speak of.

Tracy made it very clear after just three days that she wanted to live with my three children and me. She didn't want to return home. I would ask Tracy, "Why would you want to leave such a luxurious home with every possible material possession one could ask for, as well as parents who love you and are concerned about you?"

She responded; "If I could live here with you, I would be happy because there is happiness in your home."

"But you have a loving home with happiness," I replied.

Tracy quickly responded, "In my home it's a controlled happiness, a false happiness. In your home there is no name-calling, screaming, or put-downs. There is peace in your house and that is happiness. Sir, I would rather live in a cardboard box and have peace than go back to my mansion. My home is beautiful on the outside, but there is a cancer on the inside."

We need to insure that we do not get caught up in false values. All our words and actions should foster gospel values. These values lead to happiness. One of these values is gratitude. Teaching our children to be grateful for whatever they have is very important. They must learn to "appreciate" rather than "expect." When they learn to appreciate and have gratitude for the smallest of blessings, they see things differently and will be much happier as a result.

While I was working with the Sisters of the Holy Trinity in Mexico, they brought me to a very special church, the church for the street kids of Mexico City. It was a small, humble building made of wood and located in a poor area. The inside of the church was simple, with wooden pews, a concrete floor, and a handmade cross. However, hanging over the altar, was a spectacular sketch of Jesus at the "scourging of the pillar." It was a pencil sketch that was so magnificent it drew me like a magnet.

I asked the old woman who was the caretaker of the church if I could buy it. She laughed and said no. I offered her five hundred dollars American and she said no. I offered one thousand dollars American and she said no. I offered her five thousand dollars American and she said no. She replied, "You can offer us all the money in the world but you still cannot have the picture. There is something in life more important than money and that is gratitude. The sketch was done by a fourteen-year-old boy and donated in gratitude to Father Pat for saving him from the streets."

I knew then that that sketch would never be for sale.

This is living gospel values. This will instill in our children the values that Jesus lived. Think about a gospel-rooted approach to living, an approach that embraces humility as one of the greatest gifts and recognizes that from humility comes gratitude and from gratitude comes charity and from charity comes happiness. We know the key to happiness does not come from material possessions; it comes from within. It is rooted in embracing the many wonderful teachings that Jesus offered each of us. This requires faith, trust, and belief in all that Jesus gave to us.

Contemplate for a moment this quote from an African living in Rwanda: "When the soul is full the stomach is never empty, and when the soul is empty the stomach is never full."

This story illustrates the "full stomach" of charity and happiness:

We were preparing for a prayer service for the entire school body. "Community: Supporting Each Other" was the theme. This prayer service was the conclusion to a fund-raising event with a goal of five thousand dollars. The aim had been to offer research money to organizations that could help find cures for illnesses that people in our community, or their families, had suffered. For example, two of our teachers had lost their young wives to cancer. Further, we had a number of students with mental health issues. Thus, part of the money would be going to the Cancer Society and to the Mental Health Association.

The fund-raiser was set up so that if we reached our goal, twenty people, consisting of staff and students, would shave off all their hair from their head. I was one of those twenty people and as a woman I have to admit, I had reservations about how I would look with a shaved head. As the week progressed, we reached the goal. The community was very proud and excited. They looked forward to the time of the head-shaving event.

At the prayer service, one of the teachers whose wife died of cancer gave an address. His talk included his great appreciation for the gesture that the community had made for him and his family. He thanked the entire community for their support and love. The crowd was in tears. Both students and staff loved this teacher and they were deeply moved to witness him speak in this way.

Following the prayer service, the fun began. Our heads were shaved. The crowd went crazy. Everyone was on their feet cheering. It was a happy and enjoyable event.

From the time of this event onward, many students began to say hello to me in the hallways. Students that I did not know complimented me on shaving my head. Others told me they loved the new look! The respect that students showed me after this event was amazing. They began offering to help me and took an active role in enhancing the faith life of the school community. I had reached students that I never dreamed of reaching through this simple act.

Many were in awe over this event and talked about it for years afterward. Witnessing people in the community who were willing to embrace a cause that was beyond them had a powerful impact. It demonstrated that reaching beyond oneself can produce meaning and joy in one's life. There is greater joy in giving than receiving!

While in the mountains of the Dominican Republic, I was blessed to work with the people of a poor village. One afternoon we sat and talked. I asked them, "What makes a person happy?"

They were taken aback by the question, as if it was a silly question and assumed that everyone is happy. Because they knew I was a teacher, they imagined me to be an intelligent man. They thought I was testing them and that I was looking for the correct answer to the question. They began the discussion, bantering back and forth in Spanish. Finally, they believed they had the answer and they told me, "If a man has his health, he has happiness."

I explained that there were many people where I came from who have their health and are unhappy. This confused them and again they discussed among themselves in order to arrive at the correct answer. After great debate, they delivered their second answer, saying, "If a man has his health and a job, then he is happy."

As disappointing as I knew it would be to them, I had to tell them that I knew many people who had their health and a good job and were still unhappy. This caused a real commotion, almost a state of chaos. It led to an even more-heated and anxious discussion among them.

Finally, they arrived at their third answer and hoped it was the right answer. They said to me, "Sir, if a man has his health and a job and is still unhappy, he must have mental problems."

We believe our youth think this way, deep down, under all the layers of propaganda placed on them. If we can tear away the materialism and false conceptions of success, we will find the innocent and pure teenager who is happy with very little and who desires to contribute much to the world in their own way through their gifts. We find a craving to live gospel values and to know that in and through this, peace, happiness, and fulfillment will be attained.

COMPUTER USE AND THE INTERNET

Our youth spend a great deal of time on computers and the Internet, using them for research, school assignments, games, instant messaging, and simply "surfing the Net." Moreover, with technological convergence, they can now access the Internet from computers they carry around in the pockets—that is, on their Internet-ready cell phones. While we recognize and appreciate that these technologies are an undeniable part of their lives, their time should not *revolve* around their computers or cell phones.

Time for research and completion of assignments is necessary. Time for some game playing, Web browsing, and instant messaging is acceptable. However, spending endless hours playing games, communicating with friends, or exploring "questionable" sites is not acceptable. Instant Messenger, and popular sites like Facebook, MySpace, and YouTube are only a few of the many avenues of communication and entertainment available to our children and students. They need to broaden their horizons. Responsible and limited use of these sites may prove beneficial, but excessive and reckless use is destructive and counterproductive.

Problems arising through irresponsible Internet use have the same implications students experience in the rest of their lives—whether from hateful language, bullying, gossip, slander, vulgarities, or the misuse of information. The scale and availability of the Internet magnify the problem, as information that was previously spread slowly among friends and classmates now can be circulated worldwide instantaneously. The consequences are far more reaching.

It is the responsibility of adults to confront and address these issues in an assertive way. In helping our children and students find meaning in their lives, we must take the time to explain to our children how spending endless hours using instant-messaging services and visiting "questionable" sites is a waste of valuable time. Furthermore, we need to have them recognize the harmful potential of these sites and activities.

To deal with these excesses, we could lobby for the creation of education courses, or units within current courses, that address the ethical, legal, and emotional implications arising from irresponsible use of the computer and Internet. We need to invite into our schools experts who are able to speak to parents, staff, and students about the problems and issues that flow from these technologies—and these experts must be able to relate to the students on "their own level." Finally, as parents and educators, we should seek to discover the particular values and sensibilities in our children that attract them to these sites and programs, and determine what actions we need to take to prevent the nurturing of values in our children that run contrary to the teachings of the gospels.

The basic issues that are at the core of irresponsible computer use provide us with "teachable moments." We can discuss with our students and children questions like

1. Is it acceptable to let others profit from the creation of sites or technologies that are harmful to others?
2. How can we implement a practical means of insuring that people are accountable—on both the individual level and the corporate level?
3. What can we do to limit the influence of potentially destructive sites and activities?

At the root of these questions lies a simple acknowledgment: *Reckless computer use does more harm than good.*

To help our children and students understand better the destructive nature of irresponsible computer use, we can share stories (on a confidential basis, without using names) where innocent people have been hurt. We can teach them the potential of the written word for causing harm. We can emphasize that once something has been *said*, it is very difficult for it to be erased, and attempts to explain often appear defensive. The Internet can destroy reputations, both locally and globally—an extremely serious consequence of irresponsible use of the written word. How does one properly recover from fallacious rumors or statements?

Once students recognize the destructive potential of the Internet, two things will be accomplished: (1) They will be encouraged to use computers and the Internet more responsibly, and (2) They will have an awareness of the need for a healthy balance. The Internet can be fun and enjoyable. However, there are far more important and worthy endeavors to which teenagers need to devote their time and attention to help them discover meaning in their lives.

In addition to the intrinsic harm from the excessive use of the Internet, and from that of playing computer/video games, parents need to recognize that these activities are extremely addictive. Many parents are simply happy to have their children entertained at home and otherwise preoccupied, but are unaware of, or do not have sufficient concern for, the consequences. Even more than television did to previous generations, computer/video games and the Internet promote a sedentary lifestyle and consequently have a deleterious effect upon the health of our children.

Parents must take an active role in monitoring and controlling their children's use of computers and the Internet. Most parents would be shocked at the vulgarity and crudeness explicitly used on instant-messaging programs. Moreover, computer/video games are becoming increasingly violent and realistic, and should be considered unacceptable for minors. Parents need to discuss issues of concern with their children, and not simply rely upon teachers to impart caution or information. Parents should remain calm and understanding, because their children may feel terribly deprived at the imposition of rules and usage-controls of the Internet and their computers. In spite of your good intentions, they may feel you are being unfair.

So, how do we manage a situation in which there seems to be no easy answer? We deal with it as we always do: by teaching values, responsibility, and obligation. We educate young people about the inherent risks that come with the technologies and discuss our concerns for the risks. We maintain an active dialogue with our children and develop and nurture a sense of ongoing faith and respect. They need to understand our expectations of them, and then we need to trust them.

DISAGREEMENTS PROVIDE OPPORTUNITIES

We need to be patient with our children. We need to recognize that they are learning through our words and actions and that this learning process takes a long time. They will often disagree with us. During these disagreements, children are processing all that is said and done. They are watching every move and assessing the importance that we, as parents and as educators, put on certain values. They are assessing the level of our commitment, the sincerity of our beliefs, and the sacrifices that we are willing to make to insure that our values are not compromised. This is an important experience for our children and students. If they witness that some values are of such importance that great sacrifices need to be made to insure that they are not compromised, and they witness us as adults making these sacrifices, they will be impacted for life.

Disagreements will also occur on simple matters, such as the rules we set and the parameters we create. Arguments will take place over such issues as length of time on the computer, evening curfews, cell-phone bills, money, and choice of friends. Points of discussion, like who they are allowing on their MySpace and Facebook pages, may seem insignificant to us, but these things are very significant to them. With the advances in modern technology and the new means of communication available to them, these disagreements are more likely to arise. We may feel at a disadvantage because we do not have a knowledge or appreciation of many of the technological tools available to them. However, we must keep in mind that in the discussions that take place on all these various issues, our children are watching us closely. They are looking for consistency in our rules, logic in our arguments, and compassion in our relationship with them. Most important is that we as educators and parents are setting an example by our every action and word. It is important that we take time to assess and evaluate our own values and insure that they are meaningful and worthy of building our life upon. This is where the gospels will help us. If we follow the example of Jesus and live out gospel values, we are providing our children with a foundation that is solid and will lead to their prosperity and happiness.

UNDERSTANDING OUR YOUTH

If we wish to help our teens, we need to better understand their way of thinking. Without such an understanding and appreciation, it will be very difficult to help them. We will become overly frustrated and even angry. We must attempt to walk in their shoes if we wish to understand and relate to them. We remember that in some ways our children think and function in a different world.

They see things differently, hear things differently, and interpret things differently. They are exposed to songs, media, technology, and advertising that is targeting them and trying to convince them of what they should wear, what they should eat, what they should think, and how they should live. We must be aware that they do not see things as we do. We must want to see the world as they see it so that we can present ideas, direction, and insight that make sense to them. We will not be able to do this unless we understand them.

The lives of many teens are often full with school, homework, chores, extracurricular activities, part-time jobs, and a very important social life. They are busy and they do not take a great deal of time to analyze their lives or themselves. This is where we can help direct and guide them. We need to spend a lot of time with them and observe them closely to be able to help them discern where they can find meaning. We must try to come to know what motivates them, what they care about, and how they see the world. Once we do this we will be better able to guide and direct them in ways that are fruitful and meaningful.

One way to help them discover meaning is to expose them to as much as possible. The time and energy spent here is well worth the effort. Help them discover things that excite them, challenge them, and make them feel good about who they are and about the gifts with which they have been blessed. Remember, the meaning in life we are helping them to discover does not have to be what *we* consider to be great. It can be as simple as providing artwork for the halls of the school, creating videos to motivate the student body for fund-raising initiatives, babysitting for someone in need, or caring for the elderly through sharing their gifts in music, art, or companionship. It may take years to discover this meaning in one's life, and for this reason we must be patient with our youth. Keep in mind that by our very effort to assist them we are providing them with comfort and support that will carry them through.

What we are setting out here is best articulated in the following words from the Gospel of Matthew, "Those who lose their life for my sake will find it" (Matt 10:39b). Even if these teens find it difficult to appreciate fully the significance of this profound text, it is important for us to keep these words in mind as we help them on their journey. They may underestimate their ability to contribute, and they may lack motivation; however, finding their meaning in life will provide them with what they need to carry them through. It will assist in jolting them onto a different path and reveal a new reality. The reality is that they have this greatness buried deep within, a greatness that reflects the beauty, wisdom, and love of their Creator. Once on this path, they are on the road to leading meaningful, fulfilling, and happy lives.

A person's reason for living is unique to them. Once we discover our own reason(s) for living, we live life with a renewed vigor, and approach every day with enthusiasm and a good spirit. We have to help each one of our troubled teens to find their meaning in life.

Dear Jesus:
Keep me steadfast in my role to nurture the gifts of [*child's name*].
Grant me the patience to work through the struggles and
    disagreements.
Keep me sensitive to the importance of my every word and action.

May all I do reflect the values that you taught
and may this be a powerful living witness to all.
Amen.

PRACTICAL TIPS

- Encourage youth to reach beyond themselves by
  responding to a need or cause that is greater than they are.
- Be willing to make sacrifices in your own life in order to
  embrace gospel values. Personal sacrifice is the best
  teaching tool for your children or students.
- Educate yourself about the use of the Internet and enter
  into discussions about it with your children.
- Do not become discouraged with disagreements; they
  provide opportunities to teach your children.
- Walk in the shoes of your child or student—attempt to live
  "a day in the life of our youth."

POINTS TO PONDER

- *Actions speak louder than words.* What do my actions say?
- *Values must be lived.* What values do I embrace? How do
  my daily actions evidence my commitment to these
  values?
- What events and activities will help our children or students reach beyond themselves? What event or activity
  am I going to organize or plan?

SPIRITUAL EXERCISES

Exercise One

Read the following, adapted from Loren Eiseley's *The Star Thrower.*

Once upon a time there was a wise man who used to go to the
ocean to do his writing. He had a habit of walking on the
beach before he began his work.

One day he was walking along the shore. As he looked down the beach, he saw a human figure moving like a dancer. He smiled to himself to think of someone who would dance to the day. So he began to walk faster to catch up.

As he got closer, he saw that it was a young man and that the young man wasn't dancing. He was reaching down, picking up something, and very gently throwing it into the ocean. As the wise man got closer he called out, "Good morning! What are you doing?"

The young man paused, looked up, and replied, "Throwing starfish in the ocean. The sun is up and the tide is going out. And if I don't throw them in, they'll die."

"But, young man, don't you realize that there are miles and miles of beach and starfish all along it. You can't possibly make a difference!"

The young man listened politely. He then bent down, picked up another starfish, threw it into the ocean past the breaking waves, and said, "It made a difference for that one."

Ask your children or students to write a one-page reflection based on the following questions: Was the man throwing the starfish back into the water doing something that was meaningful? Why or why not? If he did this every day, would he be leading a meaningful life? How do we as society measure what is meaningful? Are we fair in our assessment?

EXERCISE TWO

Ask your children or students to create a time line for themselves. Ask them to record significant events or remarkable experiences that they believe have been important in their life, from their birth to the current date.

Then ask them to write a one-page reflection on one of the events on the time line and explain its significance in their lives. Why was it significant? What do they remember most about it? Did it change them in any way?

Chapter Four

CREATE OPPORTUNITIES FOR THEM

For we are what God has made us, created in Christ Jesus for good works, which God prepared beforehand to be our way of life. (Eph 2:10)

We begin this chapter by sharing a story:

During a poster contest in our school, a student brought in a wonderful piece of work. His talent was immediately recognizable. I asked to see more. He brought me cartooning work he had done over the years that was so brilliant I felt compelled to submit it to a world-famous cartoon book company in New York.

They were very impressed. They contacted me and requested a meeting with the boy. The boy's parents refused. They had different plans for their son. They did not think cartoon drawing was a suitable or stable career. They believed nothing significant would happen if their son chose cartooning as a career. They wanted him to work in the family variety store. Little did they know!

Perhaps a fear of failure, a lack of confidence, or a basic distrust in our teens' abilities makes us reluctant to give them the opportunities that can make them great. Whatever the reason, opportunities as great as this one come along rarely in life. Tragically, when they do, we too often let them slip away. For teenagers, they come along even less, often due to our reluctance to provide them with an opportunity.

Provide and create opportunities for teenagers. It is hard work that challenges our creativity and requires insight. At times, it will involve taking risks. However, it will pay off. In most cases, our youth will surprise us with just how capable they are and with the great things they can accomplish.

Even when they fail at a project, they will continue to impress us by how much they have learned and the growth that has taken place within them.

Jesus had great faith in the young men he chose as apostles. He chose men that most of us would never dream of choosing. Peter was a wild-tempered, unpredictable, and an aggressive young man. Simon was a zealot, attacking and killing Romans in the night. Jesus even chose Paul, a man who captured Christians and had them imprisoned and killed. Jesus gave to each of these men, as well as to the women he chose to have with him, an opportunity to accentuate their greatness. This opportunity he offered was an invitation. None of them were forced. In spite of their weaknesses, and perhaps his own fear of their potential failures, he believed in them and did not hesitate to give them this opportunity.

Patricia was a very enthusiastic, ambitious, and intelligent girl. However, she lacked social skills. She found it difficult to get along with her peers and, although she was a good student, she often clashed with her teachers and fellow students. She tried to get involved in a number of groups and school activities but met with numerous problems. She was stubborn at times, single-minded, and aggressive. It may have been these qualities that prevented her from getting along with her peers, especially when they worked on projects together or when she was part of a school group.

She had just become a sophomore, and so, counting that year, had three more years before graduating. I wanted to get her to work on her social skills and to learn to work cooperatively and productively with others. Three more years of friction would hinder her growth, make high school a traumatic experience, and ultimately, affect her postsecondary education and adult life. I believed her intelligence, creativity, ambition, and even her stubbornness and aggressiveness, had marked Patricia for great things to come.

I didn't believe that making her a part of a school group would be productive. She had already been a part of a couple of school groups and it just didn't work out. I decided to take a risk and make Patricia chairperson of a major fund-raising project in the school. Her job was to organize a committee of student volunteers that would run an evening of entertainment. It involved working with students, teachers, parents, and performers. The task was set and she had the opportunity to take her abilities and do something of significance.

Given Patricia's reputation for being difficult to work with, a number of staff and students voiced criticism for this decision to give her a position of authority and responsibility. They anticipated friction and chaos. They didn't realize that this opportunity would enable her to utilize her gifts. This leadership role would enable her to rise to greater heights.

Success meant so much to her in this new task that it forced her to curb some of her excesses. As a result, she grew. Now she was more than part of the group—she was its leader. This gave her the opportunity to change her ways to meet with success. It created enough pressure to launch the painful process of inner change because achieving something great meant more to Patricia than the comfort of the familiar. The responsibility of her role pushed her to examine her faults because if she did not, the project would collapse around her.

Now, there was no shortage of problems throughout the project. Patricia often clashed with staff and her fellow volunteers. I could see the inner struggle unfolding. We attempted to promote in her qualities of leadership through humility, flexibility, and service. She was challenged to see that great leaders are people who serve rather than desire to be served. She gradually realized that being abrasive did not work. She became empathetic toward her fellow workers, putting herself in their shoes in order to understand why they responded the way they did. She was challenged to be democratic in her leadership.

Although painful, Patricia eventually changed her ways. The project was a great success. For Patricia, her success was twofold. The school community was pleased with the significant amount of money she raised but, more importantly, they began to see Patricia in a new light. Instead of being viewed as abrasive and difficult, Patricia was now seen as capable and even "cool."

This opportunity guided Patricia to learn new ways of communicating, leading, and directing. She learned to work with others by leading collaboratively. It helped her to discover her strengths and abilities and to identify and begin to address her weaknesses. Ultimately, it made her feel better about herself.

It is important to create situations and organize events that provide teenagers the opportunity to do something great. We should not be afraid to let our young people respond to opportunities. We must be courageous, take risks, and demonstrate unwavering confidence in them. Even the roughest and toughest kids can surprise us with their capabilities and their willingness to take on a challenge. It is our confidence in them, coupled with their own talent, which will ultimately bring success.

As you walk this journey with them, remain one step behind them, never beside or in front of them. We are there to pick them up if they fall or to nudge them when they hesitate. Allow them to lead and let them know they are an inspiration to us.

The following story demonstrates the importance of balancing our own fears with providing opportunity for our teens:

It was exam time. Summer was upon us and students were anxious to be free of school. Anxious and rambunctious students congregated in my office. One of the students had brought in a DVD player and a movie. He wanted to watch a movie in my office with his friends before an exam. The problem was that I had a scheduled appointment outside the building. School policy was such that I could not leave students unattended in my office, yet I didn't feel comfortable asking them to leave. The student who had brought in the DVD player took me aside and asked if he and his friends could stay.

He was a beautiful boy who always went out of his way to help. However, I feared they would get themselves and me into trouble. I said to him privately, "Okay, Matthew, but you are in charge. If there are any problems, I will hold you responsible." I announced that I was leaving, listed some rules for the kids, and informed them that Matthew was in charge.

When I returned, the students had left to write their exam. My office looked different. It was cleaner. All the chairs were returned to their places, the garbage had been emptied, and the desks and couch tidied. The place looked great. Instantly, I panicked. I imagined the students being blasted by administration and being told to clean up.

I nervously waited for students or staff to come in and break the news that the students had misbehaved and were now in trouble. A half hour later, Matthew returned. "Hi, Miss," he said. "How was your meeting?"

"Great," I replied. Matthew just smiled. "Did everything go okay?" I asked.

"Yeah, great, Miss."

"Who cleaned the place up?" I asked.

"Oh, I did that," he answered offhandedly. "Do you like it?"

We must believe in our youth so that they can believe in themselves. We must not let our own fear of failure prevent us from providing them with opportunities. We have all seen the bravery of young people in times of war, their creativity in works of art, their compassion in times of need, and their hope in times of despair. We don't have to wait for wars or world disasters to call upon them to use their gifts. Life will present many opportunities to empower our teenagers.

Try not to rule out teenagers who present a rough-and-tough exterior. Often we have selected the most unlikely students to act as ministers during prayer services. This is not easy. They frequently resist, and we must be creative in gaining their cooperation. When they do cooperate, they surprise themselves with how much they enjoy leading the community in a spiritual service. We believe this experience also reveals to them their own spirituality. In fact, their spiritual depth might amaze and perplex them. These seemingly "unholy" kids can successfully and faithfully lead a congregation of 1,800 kids in prayer. This brief experience can bear long-term fruit. They will begin to see the greatness and goodness within themselves because others have witnessed it in them.

The key in this process is patience. We must be patient. The Sisters of the Holy Trinity, in Mexico, taught me about being patient with teenagers.

While working with the sisters, I observed and marveled at the wonderful work they did with the young girls in their missions. However, there was one evening I find particularly fascinating. As I sat and talked with a number of the sisters, I observed off in the distance, at the end of the room, an older sister working with one of the younger girls.

The older sister worked for two hours with this young teenager, unraveling a ball of thread. It was completely tangled and knotted. It now had to be unraveled and spooled again to be reused. Thread was important in the mission because sewing was taught as an important trade.

I watched in disbelief as the two of them worked calmly and patiently at unraveling the ball. They talked and laughed enjoying each other's company. Occasionally they would look up at me and the other sisters and give us a smile.

I returned to my room that night to reflect on our work in the streets with the poor and the unraveling of the thread. I realized as I reflected and read scriptures that the older sister was teaching the young girl something much more valuable than saving a few pennies by saving the thread. She was teaching her patience and appreciation. She was teaching her that the simplest of works, done with appreciation and patience, can be rewarding and fun.

As a parent or educator, take the steps necessary to provide your teens opportunities for greatness. Do not be afraid to take chances. Pray for patience and confront the traditional norms with courage. When your teenager begins to see the greatness that resides within, transformation will ensue.

Dear God:
We pray for the insight to recognize opportunities for our young
    people.
If there are no appropriate opportunities,
may we have the creativity and the wisdom to create ones
that will inspire and encourage our young people.
Grant us confidence in our young people
so that we can empower them to embrace opportunity
and experience the joy of success and achievement.
Grant us the patience to work with them
and to endure all the difficulties and obstacles.
Amen.

PRACTICAL TIPS

- Do not let your own fears limit the opportunities you
  create for teens.
- Build them up! Be a constant source of encouragement,
  particularly when they fall.
- Impress upon them the importance of trying and risking.
  Instill in them that their effort builds their character.

POINTS TO PONDER

- What do you think of when you see a young person with
  pink hair walking down the street or walking down the
  hallway at school?
- Do you let your impressions of people effect the
  opportunities you offer them?
- Jesus created opportunities for people many would
  question—people like Peter and Paul. Would you create
  opportunities for people like Peter and Paul?

SPIRITUAL EXERCISES

EXERCISE ONE

Paul worked closely with the religious leaders of his time to have Christians imprisoned and killed (see Acts of the Apostles 8:1–3). Paul seemed to be a most unlikely candidate to be chosen to serve Jesus. Yet, Jesus appeared to him and offered to him a whole new world and an opportunity to take on a whole new life (Acts 9:1–22).

Review the following questions with your children or students:

1. Why would the Lord have given this opportunity to a person like Paul?
2. Do you think Paul made the right choice, given that he suffered martyrdom twelve years later?
3. Do you see opportunities coming to *you* in life, even though you may consider yourself unworthy or unable? What are these opportunities and how did you or do you respond?

EXERCISE TWO

1. Ask your children or students to list five things that they would like to attain, either in the school or in the community. These may be programs they wish to initiate, tasks they wish to accomplish, or policies they wish to have put into effect.
2. After they answer this question, ask them what the obstacles are that they face that prevent them from attaining these things.
3. Finally, ask what they or others in their life can do to make their goals attainable.

Chapter Five
_____

CHALLENGE THEM

"The kingdom of heaven is like a mustard seed that someone took and sowed in his field; it is the smallest of all the seeds, but when it has grown it is the greatest of shrubs and becomes a tree, so that birds of the air come and make nests in its branches." (Matt 13:31–32)

_____

Joseph was fourteen years old, in grade nine, and in trouble at school. He was a short, handsome, Italian boy with tremendous energy. However, his energy was being channeled in the wrong direction. Joseph's infractions and the rough group of kids he was associating with concerned the vice principal. She was worried about Joseph's behavior and choices. She knew he was on the wrong path and she wanted to redirect him. For the latest infraction, she decided that rather than suspend him for three days, she would force him to work with the school chaplain. For Joseph, time with the school chaplain would be a form of penance. He had no choice but to comply.

In our first meeting, I learned a great deal about Joseph. He was intelligent, energetic, and very sociable. However, he was confused and bored with school. Moreover, he suffered with an inner desire to live up to his own expectations. Coming from a family of successful lawyers, businesspersons, and politicians, Joseph's expectations of himself were quite high. He needed to feel he was a "somebody" and that he was accomplishing something.

I believed Joseph's expectations of himself were unrealistic and unfair. They created within him anxiety and confusion that led to inappropriate behavior. Doing well in school was not enough for Joseph. He believed anyone could do well in school. He wanted to do more. His compulsion begged for further study but something needed to be done immediately to help correct his inappropriate behavior. Joseph needed to be challenged.

During our third meeting, I told Joseph I believed that he was a kid with great gifts, that he had the potential to do great things, and that life was challenging him to live up to his potential. Joseph was reluctant to accept compliments but was willing to continue our sessions. This was a paradox. On one hand, he had great expectations of himself and would not be satisfied unless he did great things. On the other hand, he was a young boy who was insecure about his own abilities and afraid of taking risks. Somewhere in this maze, Joseph found deviant behavior as a channel for his frustrations.

During our next visit, I told Joseph that he was needed to help with a major fund-raiser for the poor in our community. He was being challenged to do something great for others. Joseph agreed to work on this project. At that moment, the seeds were sown for a wonderful journey for Joseph.

Over the next four years, Joseph accomplished many positive and wonderful things. He successfully ran for student council. He served two years as treasurer and in his final year was elected president. He worked on numerous fund raisers, raising thousands of dollars for the poor in our community. Community organizations solicited Joseph to sit on their boards. He was the recipient of numerous awards, including a gold medal for being an outstanding student. He was the subject of articles in local newspapers, received scholarships to college, and became a role model for, and mentor to, other kids.

Joseph initially made some poor choices. We see this repeatedly in our young people. We wonder why wonderful kids make poor choices and get involved in negative and destructive behavior. A poor self-image, problems at home, peer pressure, simple boredom, or the need for excitement can spark poor behavior. Perhaps they know that deep down inside, despite their insecurities, they are capable of great things. What they need is to be challenged!

When Jesus approached the man who could not walk and had spent his life on a mat, he said to him, "Stand up, take your mat and walk" (John 5:8). With these words, Jesus challenged him to find the courage to get up and walk. This man had spent his entire life on a mat and as much as he wanted to walk, he had become "comfortable" on that mat.

Likewise, sometimes our teenagers become "comfortable" in the world they are in, because they are afraid to venture out. Insecurity prevents them from taking the chance and leaving the world in which they are comfortable. It is understandable for someone to become comfortable with chaos and misery when all they have known is chaos and misery. We may all find comfort in an uncomfortable state if we are familiar with it. We may want out, but are hesitant to abandon that which we know; we hesitate to embrace change.

Many of our teenagers have become comfortable with the lives they are living. It may be an unproductive or destructive life, but it is what they have come to know. It has become their comfort zone. Yet they are aware, deep inside themselves, that there is something better and they desire that better life. They need to be challenged, to be given the courage to "get up and walk."

How do we appropriately challenge our youth? First, we turn to arguably one of their most powerful influences—their friends. They love their friends and go to great lengths to support, protect, and stand up for them. They listen to their friends, take their advice, and follow their lead. For this reason, developing healthy friendships is extremely important. It is crucial that they choose friends who are going to challenge them and give them courage to live that better life.

We cannot tell our children who their friends should be but we can guide and direct them. We can encourage them to foster friendships that bring out the best in them. We can emphasize the importance of friends who lead us to success, elevate us, make us feel good about doing good, instill courage, and present challenges. We can use the example of our own friends in guiding our children and students; sharing situations in which the great qualities of our own friends enabled us to get through the difficult times and encouraged us in our success. Some say that we are only as successful as those with whom we associate. So, encourage your children or students to choose friends who elevate them to a higher ground and impress upon them the importance of doing the same with *their* friends.

Unfortunately, some of our children have chosen friends who pose a negative influence on them and who cause them to make poor choices, create a lower self-image, and encourage them to channel their energy in the wrong direction.

Maria was a beautiful sixteen-year-old girl who had been dating a boy for over a year. Maria's parents were very concerned about the boy she was dating. He would bring her home late at night, he liked to drink, and they knew he was taking drugs. They actually liked the boy but did not like his lifestyle. The parents decided that it was best to separate Maria from him. Maria knew his behavior lacked proper judgment at times, yet she was too attached to end their relationship. Maria's parents decided the best solution was for her to live with her father a few hundred kilometers away. Maria agreed.

One weekend while Maria was visiting her mother, the boy called and asked her to go out. A group of teens were going out together, and the mother knew them. She reluctantly agreed after receiving assurances from Maria that she would be safe.

At 10:00 p.m., Maria called her mother to assure her all was well and that she loved her. At 11:00 p.m., Maria's mother got a phone call saying there had been a terrible accident and that she should come to the hospital. When her mother reached the hospital, she was told Maria was dead. She died on impact when the car her boyfriend was driving hit a utility pole. All the others in the car, including the boyfriend, survived. The boy was convicted of drinking and driving. In the lawsuits that followed, evidence was produced that he had also taken drugs. He served time in jail.

Maria's parents were devastated. Their pain and suffering continue to this day. Maria's mother remains involved with MADD (Mothers Against Drunk Driving) and has given talks to caution young people about drinking and driving. It is painful for her to share her story, but she hopes it will prevent others from suffering the same loss. They will forever mourn the loss of their beautiful, loving daughter.

This is an example of parents taking serious action out of love for their daughter. It was not easy to take a sixteen-year-old girl and send her to live in another city or state. They were right to take such action, as the influence of this boy on their daughter was harmful and turned out to be fatal. Unfortunately, their love, support, and prudent actions could not prevent this tragedy. As parents, there are times we can do all the right things, but bad things still happen. The important point is that we are doing all we can to help our children be set on the right path.

We can create challenges for our youth as a parent or educator. We must be creative and present challenges beyond the daily routines of cutting grass, taking the attendance sheet to the office, or doing laundry. We have to challenge them to perform great acts. Present a teenager with the right challenge, and it will excite and motivate them and instill confidence. Further, it demonstrates that *we* believe in *them*. It will cause rushes of adrenalin and give them something toward which they can direct their boundless, youthful energy. Such a challenge will make them feel valued and valuable. "The good person brings good things out of a good treasure" (Matt 12:35a). The challenge will push them to yet-greater heights. It will become an opportunity to prove to themselves and to others that they are important and that they have talents that are worthy of praise.

I was planning a prayer service for our school community and was looking for a guest speaker who could impress upon students and staff the importance of service. I chose the theme "Pay It Forward," based upon the movie of the same name, which had been released recently. I invited a student named James to be our speaker. He was a class clown who suffered from Tourette's syndrome. James was an unlikely choice. Yet I challenged him to draft a speech and it was apparent that he was excited by the challenge.

He returned to my office a few days later to share his speech with me. I asked him to read it as though he was delivering it to the school. He was nervous and rigid in his delivery—his personality nowhere to be found. Careful not to show my disappointment, I asked him to redraft the speech and to try to make it more his own, to insure that his personality was reflected in its content and delivery. I worried about whether he had the confidence in himself to tackle the task.

Two days later, he returned to my office. He delivered the speech and I was delighted and amazed. He had made the speech his own and delivered it in a manner that reflected his personality.

Giving his talk at the service, James provoked both laughter and tears in students and staff. He did a superb job and received a standing ovation. His speech was powerful and memorable. He had risen to the challenge!

Finding the appropriate challenge is not always easy. There may be numerous trials and errors. If you have a teenager who does not respond to challenges involving academics, athletics, or entrepreneur ventures, try the area of service to others. Get them working for charities, feeding the poor, caring for the aged or the sick, or spending time with the homeless. Present a challenge that will stir the great love and sensitivity they have within. Rest assured, all teenagers have this love within. Young people have a sense of justice and an instinctive concern for the underdog. Lead them to this work and they will gain confidence and be empowered.

If we accept the premise that it is through self-sacrifice and giving to others that we experience true joy, then our teenagers will discover that joy when they take on such challenges. In their act of greatness, they will discover how much they are needed in a broken world and the extent to which they can help heal the brokenness. These acts that heal the world will lead them to heal themselves.

These teenagers, in their success, realize that it is not the teen that needs the challenge but rather the challenge that needs the teen. We needed James to write and deliver that speech. He realized through his own experiences the special gifts he possessed. He was awakened from his slumber, found the courage to take on the challenge, and in doing so, he discovered his greatness.

We must exercise good judgment in finding the right challenge for each of our children and students. If we study the child—their interests, strengths, gifts, and personality—we will be able to set an appropriate challenge. We must stay with them throughout the process, letting them know that we are there for them and believe in them. Our confidence in them will give them confidence in themselves. If they do not succeed, do not be discouraged. Soldier on with challenges that are more suitable. Our actions, our trust, and our efforts will help to transform these children.

> Dear God:
> Help us as we work with [*child's name*].
> May we provide a challenge at which [*he/she*] will succeed.
> May this experience offer [*child's name*] confidence in [*his/her*] ability
> to accomplish great things in this world.
> May our trust in [*him/her*] and may our desire to help add to [*his/her*] success.
> May the goodness that exists in [*child's name*] be revealed,
> and may we be directed by the Spirit to help reveal this goodness.
> Amen.

PRACTICAL TIPS

- Think BIG in offering challenges. Youth are extremely talented.
- Take the time to contemplate the children's or students' gifts and strengths and offer challenges that will bring out these gifts.
- Help create healthy friendships, which will help create healthy children—do all you can to nurture healthy friendships for your children or students.
- Be confident in our youth and you help them build up their own confidence in themselves. Demonstrate your confidence in their abilities.

48

POINTS TO PONDER

At the age of twelve, Craig Kielburger from Thornhill, Ontario, read an article about a young boy in Pakistan who was sold into slavery to work in a carpet factory. Craig gathered together a small group of his grade-seven classmates and Free the Children was born.

The following year, at the age of thirteen, Craig went to South Asia to witness for himself child slave labor. He held a press conference and the world was made aware of the plight of these children. In addition to Free the Children, Kielburger cofounded Leaders Today and is the recipient of many international awards and honors for his work defending children's rights.

- Contemplate the accomplishments of our youth. Look at Craig Kielburger who, at twelve, decided he wanted to make a difference. What enables our youth to "make a difference"?
- What challenges are available to offer our students and children in our schools and community?
- What challenges can you create that will enable your children/students to shine?

SPIRITUAL EXERCISES

EXERCISE ONE

For this exercise you will need the following materials:

a one-gallon Mason jar
about twelve fist-sized rocks or stones
gravel
sand
water

Hide all ingredients.
1. Take out the Mason jar and take the rocks one at a time and put them into the jar until the rocks fill the jar to the top. Then ask your children or students: "Is it full?"

2. Take the gravel, pour it into the jar, and shake it so that it disperses throughout the jar. Then ask: "Is it full now?"
3. Then take the sand, pour it into the jar, and ask: "Is it full now?"
4. Then take the water, pour it into the jar, and ask: "What do you think is the point of this exercise?" You may get different answers, including "No matter how full your schedule is, you can always fit more things in." That is *not* the answer. If you get this answer, you may say: "That is what society may want you to believe, but it is not the answer."
5. Reveal: The point of this exercise is to demonstrate that if you don't put the big rocks in first, you will never get them in at all.
6. Ask your children and students to respond to these questions:

- What are the "big rocks" in your life? Time with family or friends, your dreams, making a difference, a worthy cause?
- How can you peal back the layers that often hide who you are to help you determine what your own rocks are? How do you think you can get to the core of your being?
- How can you insure that those things that define you, "your rocks," are a priority in your life? How can you insure that the "little things" do not prevent you from becoming who you really are?

EXERCISE TWO

1. Discuss with your children or students how Jesus invites the apostles to follow him. He does not force them. Rather, he invites them (read Mark 1:16–20). Confirm how he also invites each one of us.
2. Read or hand out the following letter from Jesus:

Dear Friend: (You may personalize each letter if you hand them out, by substituting the student's name for the word *friend*.)

I just had to send you a note to tell you how much I love you and care for you. I saw you yesterday as you were talking to your friends. I waited all day hoping you would want to talk with me.

As evening came, I gave you a sunset to close your day and a breeze to give you rest and I waited. You have no idea how much I long to hear from you. It hurts me when I do not hear from you, but I still love you because I am your friend.

I saw you fall asleep last night and I longed to touch your face. Again I waited, wanting to rush down so we could talk. You got up late and rushed off to school.

Today you looked like something was troubling you. I was hoping you would talk to me. I would love to help you. I love you! I try to tell you in the blue sky and in the quiet green grass. I whisper it in the leaves and in the trees, and I breathe it in the colors of the flowers. I showed it to you in the majesty of the mountains and in the love songs of the birds. I warm you with sunshine and sweeten the air with nature scents.

My love for you is deeper than the ocean and bigger than the biggest want or need in your heart. If you only knew how much I want to walk and talk with you. I know how hard it is on earth. I really know! And I want to help you. I want you to meet my Father. He wants to help you too. My Father is that way, you know. Just call me—ask me—talk with me! I am always waiting to hear from you.

With Love, Jesus.

3. Ask your children or students to respond to the following:

- What is Jesus offering you?
- What obstacles do you face on a daily basis that prevent you from responding to Jesus' invitation?
- How can you overcome these obstacles?
- What concrete steps are you going to take to respond to this invitation?

Chapter Six

CREATE A SENSE OF BELONGING

"Which one of you, having a hundred sheep and losing one of them, does not leave the ninety-nine in the wilderness and go after the one that is lost until he finds it? When he has found it, he lays it on his shoulder and rejoices. And when he comes home, he calls together his friends and neighbors, saying to them, 'Rejoice with me, for I have found my sheep that was lost.'" (Luke 15:4–6)

Parents approached me about their son Paul. They had noticed a change in his behavior when he turned twelve and had experienced problems with him ever since. At fifteen, he left home to live with his girlfriend. Paul and his girlfriend received welfare and were involved in drugs and crime. After a couple of years, their relationship soured and Paul returned home with the intention of straightening out his life. Having been hurt many times by Paul's lies, his parents had great difficulty trusting him. The parents and their youngest son, Steve, resented Paul, whose lifestyle had torn the family apart in many ways and caused them much grief. They blamed him for destroying the unity and cohesiveness that once existed in their home. They found it difficult to forgive him and to believe that he was sincere about starting over.

I met with Paul for four one-hour sessions. He was a beautiful young man with obvious energy and talent. He had great potential. During our sessions, it became obvious that Paul's parents were highly ambitious and career-driven. Also, Paul's brother Steve was an A student, eager to learn and busy with career-oriented activities. Steve and his parents all had interests, passions, and ambitions. Paul did not, and this made him feel different and excluded from his family.

Although very bright, Paul found school boring and frustrating. He also found himself at odds with modern notions of success. At home, he did not fit into conversations and activities, nor did he share his family's philosophy of life, success, or aspirations. Paul always felt lost and out of place. He had no reason to be in school, socially or scholastically, and no reason to be part of his family. To Paul, it seemed as if everyone had their place but him. He had no sense of belonging.

He searched desperately for a place to belong, which was why he had turned to his girlfriend and her friends who lived on the street. They offered him commonality. They shared similar feelings and could understand his struggle. They too felt they had little in common with their families and the wider world.

Paradoxically, brokenness bound these young people together. They shared a common belief that they had no reason to exist and no place to belong to. These shared experiences and feelings forged strong bonds between them.

The problem with existing in such a fraternity is that there is no direction. A fraternity that is rooted in "not belonging" does not, at a conscious level, look for a way to belong within society. Neither is there a vision or mission that holds the group together. Instead, there is only comfort in the shared experience of "not belonging." Despite the fact that wanting to belong is a basic human drive, group members function in a state of mutual discontent, which becomes their comfort zone.

This group dynamic leads to a path of destruction: crime, drug addiction, and other harmful acts. Despite strong bonds of loyalty within the group, this dynamic does not foster integrity or wholeness within its members. The group is based on brokenness. Members look to each other to fill their sense of emptiness. Yet, each is incapable of fulfilling that emptiness.

As is the case with so many young people, Paul's situation was not the fault of his parents. As parents, we tend to question our child-rearing skills and style, often blaming ourselves. Paul's parents loved him dearly and devoted a great deal of time and attention to him. They had endured tremendous pain and exercised great patience. They are spiritual, loving, dedicated people who worked tirelessly to discover Paul's life interests and to foster within him a sense of belonging and purpose. Yet, Paul was different. This is difficult for the family and the larger community who both found it difficult to fully understand and accept.

To fully appreciate Paul's experience and that of many others like him, try to imagine yourself living in a world where you feel you do not fit. Everyone seems to have a place but you. You are like a wandering nomad, searching for a place to call home. You see others connect and enjoy time together. You see them laugh and cry together, relating effortlessly. You appear to belong but you do not. You feel alienated and alone. If you are unable to imagine this, try recalling a dinner party you attended where you had nothing in common with the other guests. All you could think about all night was getting home. When you left, you felt great relief. Now, imagine there was no such escape. There was no comfort to be had at home. Imagine having no reprieve and nowhere to turn. Imagine being permanently trapped in a situation of great discomfort and alienation.

In our prison system, repeat offenders are common. Convicts will serve their time and be released, only to return to jail on new charges. Many subconsciously commit new crimes in order to return to jail, where they experience a sense of comfort and belonging in a familiar, predictable environment. Inmates come to view each other like family, forging ties based on their mutual brokenness. But these ties are not healthy. They do not have a solid foundation. Similarly, within cults and street culture, they feed off the emptiness in each other, and when you belong to emptiness, you don't really belong to anything. Eventually, such relationships will collapse.

Paul's world eventually collapsed with his adopted street family and he returned home. Yet the challenge in adjusting is not for Paul alone but for his parents and brother as well.

As in the parable of the Prodigal Son, the father and mother must greet their son with love, open arms, celebration, and a willingness to resume their journey together. They, including their other son, Steve, must be willing to forgive and to actually celebrate Paul's return. If they hold on to bitterness, anger, or mistrust, healing cannot occur.

In my meetings with Paul, we had three objectives: first, to identify and demonstrate that Paul had great talents and abilities; second, to point out to him that there was nothing wrong with feeling different and out of place; third, to let him know that there was a healthy place for him in the world where he was needed and where his identity would be validated.

We discussed together many great people who took a lifetime before discovering their love and their place in life. Yet, through patience, hard work, and determination, people do find their niche in life and with it a sense of belonging. Through persistence, they succeed and come to discover where they belong and they find peace in their world.

Paul realized that there are no easy answers. Some of the greatest minds in history, such as Thomas Aquinas and Albert Einstein, rarely experienced a sense of belonging. In fact, some of the great people in history were victims of ridicule and persecution by colleagues, family, friends, and society. However, when they discovered their gifts and how to use them, the world suddenly belonged to them.

Within three months of returning home, Paul enrolled in a college tech program. He wasn't interested in the course but realized that he had to do something to earn a living. It would buy him time until he found his niche. He also took on a number of part-time jobs, trying different things that might lead him to discovering his niche.

Being productive and proactive, Paul began to feel better. The only difference between Paul then and now is that today he is willing to be patient. He acknowledges that he is talented and gifted and that it is only a matter of time before his life passion and his place in the world are discovered.

Each child has a "reason to be" and belongs somewhere. No matter how contrary their attitudes, how odd their appearance, or how rebellious their behavior, every child has a "reason to be" and a place to be. There is a function and a place for them in this world. They are a part of God's plan and God knows each of them intimately. "And even all the hairs of your head are all counted" (Matt 10:30).

The irony is that kids like Paul, who march to a different drummer, often become leaders in business or in society. For years they feel as if they don't belong, and then the day comes when they are so successful that everyone wants to belong to them. We need to be patient and understanding. We can never find their "reason to be" or where it is they belong, but we can help them find it. We have to let them know that we support them along the way, even when they tackle nontraditional ventures. It is important to remind them that it is their uniqueness that makes this an interesting, fascinating, and glorious world.

Brad was a mature student who returned to school after years on the street. He sat in my office and sobbed uncontrollably as he shared his wayward past. Like Paul, he too felt as if he had never belonged at school or at home. This led him to join a chapter of an international biker gang where he was made a hit man.

As a teenager, he was exposed to a dangerous and violent lifestyle that he knew was wrong. Yet the fraternity and sense of belonging the gang offered were stronger than the emptiness and loneliness he felt when he lived in traditional society. It was not until one of the other bikers was shot and died in his arms that he realized that, although he had a valued sense of belonging to the group, it was a group that cultivated destruction and death.

It took this traumatic experience to make Brad resolve to turn his life around and to look elsewhere in society for his niche.

Thankfully, the journey is not as severe for most young people who simply feel out of place. These students will look for a place in the school where they will not be judged, where they can voice their opinions without being ridiculed, and where they can be themselves without feeling insecure. These are places where they are encouraged to share their insights, offer their ideas, and work to make the world a better place. They have great things to offer the world but are like young birds learning how to fly. When they take flight they are truly amazing. There are special educators that will provide for them that place of comfort and we must support every effort to create such places.

The Sisters of the Holy Trinity would go out of their way into the streets of Mexico to make sure every child "belonged." I felt a real sense of belonging with these kids when we would visit them.

These kids lived in hovels, under bridges, and in the sewers. There was always an open invitation for them to enter the mission. Many of them were so addicted to drugs, street life, and/or prostitution, it was a difficult decision for them to make. The sisters would not try to convince them to enter. The sisters would go out everyday to check on them, counsel them, teach them, and offer them food and comfort. They made the kids feel as if they were a part of the family. The kids were in rough shape emotionally, psychologically, and hygienically.

However, before we ate together on the streets, the kids always insisted on praying. We would gather in a circle, put our arms around each other, and pray. In the midst of their chaos and suffering, they saw that it was important to pray. It was important to them that we be a family, sharing together in prayer, forged in our compassion for each other, and bound by a common vision for a better life.

Yes, a sense of belonging.

We must try to do all we can to offer encouragement, support, and guidance to our children and students. Whether we are with these kids at home, in the community, or in schools, we must work to offer them what they need so they gain a sense of belonging. We know that once they have a feeling of belonging, they will become motivated and energized. In helping them feel that they belong, we help them to discover their "reason to be." We can then sit back and witness the wonderful things they do and the great people they become.

> Dear Jesus:
> We know that many in this world feel as though they do not
>   belong.
> They feel isolated, alone, and out of place.
> Help us to understand better these children and to reach out to
>   them.
> May we have insight into their feelings
> and create opportunities that assist these children in finding their
>   way.
> May we follow your example in reaching out to others who are not
>   accepted.
> Just as your love was revealed in all you did for them,
> may our actions reveal your unconditional love.
> Grant us the direction, patience, and confidence to journey with
>   these children,
> provide for them a place where they belong,
> and give them a new beginning.
> Amen.

PRACTICAL TIPS

- Remember that *each* child "belongs" because they are a part of God's creation.
- Create healthy environments, particularly in schools, where students can "be themselves."
- Remind youth that many successful people struggled to "belong." However, eventually the world belonged to them.

POINTS TO PONDER

- What does it mean "to belong"?
- Where and when is your child or student most comfortable?
- Do you think Einstein felt he belonged?

SPIRITUAL EXERCISES

Exercise One

1. Have your children or students draw a picture of "the place"
   in the world where they find themselves most comfortable.
2. Ask them to describe why they chose the place they did.

Exercise Two

1. Read the following poem to your children or students:

"Please Hear What I'm Not Saying"

Don't be fooled by me.
Don't be fooled by the face I wear,
for I wear a mask, a thousand masks,
masks that I'm afraid to take off,
and none of them is me.

Pretending is an art that's second nature with me,
but don't be fooled,
for God's sake, don't be fooled.
I give you the impression that I'm secure,...
that confidence is my name and coolness my game,...
and that I need no one,
but don't believe me....

I'm afraid that deep-down I'm nothing
and that you will see this and reject me.

So I play my game, my desperate pretending game....
I tell you everything that's really nothing,
and nothing of what's everything....
Please listen carefully and try to hear what I'm not saying....

You've got to hold out your hand
even when that's the last thing I seem to want....
Only you can call me into aliveness.

I want you to know that.
I want you to know how important you are to me....

It will not be easy for you....
The nearer you approach to me
the blinder I may strike back....
I fight against the very thing I cry out for.
But I am told that love is stronger than strong walls
and in this lies my hope.

Who am I, you may wonder?
I am someone you know very well.
For I am every man you meet
and I am every woman you meet.

Charles C. Finn

2. Choose one of the following:
   a) Ask your children or students to write a reflection on this poem. Do they think it is accurate? Do they like it? Why? Why not?
   b) Ask your children or students to draw and/or describe some of the masks they wear. If you have clay, you can ask your students to mold or shape the mask.
3. Invite them to draw or describe themselves with no mask.
4. Discuss: Are they able to do this? Why? Why not?

Chapter Seven

HELP THEM DISCOVER THEIR TALENTS AND PASSIONS

> We have gifts that differ according to the grace given to us:
> prophecy, in proportion to faith; ministry, in ministering; the
> teacher, in teaching; the exhorter, in exhortation; the giver, in
> generosity; the leader, in diligence; the compassionate, in
> cheerfulness. (Rom 12:6–7)

Every teenager has a unique talent. We have never met a teenager who was not gifted or talented in some way. Many have talents that are obviously shared by others in the world. However, when you combine that talent with a teenager's unique personality and personal life history, it becomes his or her own unique talent. Believing that every teenager has a talent is realistic. The problem is trying to find the talent and, once you have found it, to determine if the talent is their passion.

The first step is to insure that the teenager believes they are talented. To do this, we must help them believe in themselves and overcome low self-esteem, if it exists. Some teenagers truly believe that they are of little value to the big world and have nothing to offer. There are many reasons for this. For some, it stems from peers who have constantly bullied them. For others, it comes from parents who have verbally abused, insulted, or emotionally neglected them. Yet for others, it results from being hardened by a cold society that measures beauty and success in a limited manner and markets products in such a way as to leave them feeling insecure and ugly. This is further fueled by an educational system that measures the gifts and abilities of teenagers in a limited way. The disciplines that are taught are limiting, and the methods of evaluation are based primarily on memory; these may not reveal the talents of our youth. Each of these obstacles makes it difficult for teenagers to believe that they have something unique and productive to offer the world. They are often disillusioned, lost, and defeated. They are led to believe they could never achieve the goals set out for them. We have to work diligently to convince our children and our students that they are, in fact, gifted and that the world awaits their gifts. This is sometimes a slow and painful process. Sometimes we have to start with the smallest of things and convince them that they did a wonderful job.

We have to go "outside the box" and see the greatness that resides within our children and students. Once we see it, we have to help *them* see it. Then we can remind them that these gifts and talents are not theirs to possess, that they have a duty and responsibility to share their talents with humanity. This is God's gift to them, and it is now their duty to share it with the world. God desires happiness for them. God has bestowed upon them their uniqueness and special talents so they may experience happiness through the great works they will do and the contributions they will make. The discovery of talents is obviously more difficult with problem teens. Their talents are often buried under insecurity, brokenness, and deviant behavior. We have to use every resource to peel away the layers. Sometimes, we have to search in subtle ways, so they do not feel pressure.

Throughout this whole process, we must remain unrelenting. It is hard work. Let's not allow failures or obstacles to get in the way. We have to talk to teachers, friends, coaches, parents, relatives, and all those who work with our child or student, both in and outside the school setting. We have to work with all these people until the pearl is discovered. Then we must observe every action and be attentive to every thing because a window may be opened in which we can peek. Sometimes, we have to look through a small window rather than a large door.

It is a difficult challenge for us adults to remain completely open-minded in this search. The talent we discover may not be the talent for which we had hoped. The talent we discover may not be the talent that our educational system or society finds worthy of merit. The talent we discover may be one that is obscure, seem unproductive, and has no practical or monetary value according to traditional measurements. We may end up discovering that their talent resides in philosophical thinking, a heightened sensitivity, keen perceptions, or a creativity that makes no promise of security or stability in the world. No matter what their talent is, it is a talent! We have discovered a treasure. It is ironical that it is often these children who possess rare and impractical gifts, that become highly successful and prosperous, and attain personal fulfillment.

61

Carson's learning disabilities were numerous. School for him was a nightmare. His parents tried everything. Most of his teachers were too impatient and those that were patient were exhausted. During one of our sessions together, I asked him if he would go with me to get coffee and then pick up a couple of items at the store that I had to get for my family. He agreed. He would agree to anything that would keep him out of class!

I had coffee; he had a hot chocolate. We then went to the local grocery store and I picked up a few grocery items. When we approached the store clerk, I watched as she rang the items through. I noticed that Carson was watching her. I couldn't understand why he was so intent on looking at her. As she packaged the groceries, the clerk and I talked briefly. Then, Carson and I made our way out of the store.

As we walked out, I heard a voice that sounded like the clerk, with the exact same pitch and inflection. I turned and looked at Carson; he stopped and looked at me. I smiled and we carried on. When we returned to the car, I asked him to mimic the clerk. At first, he was reluctant but eventually he agreed. He imitated her voice and mannerism to a tee. His accuracy was uncanny. What was even more amazing was his ability to pick up on her idiosyncrasies. Small facial expressions and the way she pronounced certain letters along with minute physical gestures—he had read these like a computer and spit them back out. He was also able to exaggerate these characteristics in a satirical way that made me laugh. These were all qualities that I noticed in the clerk subconsciously but would never have been able to recall.

When we returned to my office, I asked him to imitate teachers and students in the school that we both knew. What I observed was nothing short of brilliant. No average person could do what he did. No brilliant student could do what he did. His perception of these qualities was so accurate it was frightening. This kid is talented! He reminded me of Jim Carrey. Perhaps he will continue to suffer in the educational system and fall short of the standards set by society. However, we know something for certain—his inability to succeed was not rooted in his lack of talent!

Some of the gifts our teens possess may even seem weird, strange, bizarre, or unbelievable. Nevertheless, they are great gifts that can help in healing a broken world.

While working in Mexico, I met a poor ninety-year-old street woman in a basilica. She was praying at one of the corner shrines.

After being introduced to her by one of the sisters, the sister then spoke with her briefly about where she had been and how she was doing. The old lady and I did not speak.

As we departed she hugged me goodbye and said she would pray for my children and me. How did she know I had children? I wasn't wearing a wedding ring. How did she know my children were presently going through a difficult time and were in need of prayer? God gives to each of us great and special gifts.

WHEN TALENTS DON'T MEET PASSIONS

Once we discover the talent, we hope that it is the teenager's passion. Some teenagers have a great talent or gift but no passion for this gift. They may be extremely gifted in academics but have no interest in it. It's difficult to understand this chemistry. One would think that the area in which they are gifted is the area in which they have their interests or passions. It makes sense to believe that this is one of the reasons why they would be gifted in that area.

However, many teenagers are gifted and yet not interested in the areas in which they are gifted. Their interest could be diminished by peer pressure, an inability to recognize value, family or societal pressures, or confusion during adolescence; or, perhaps, it could be that their passion simply lay elsewhere. It is difficult to understand and can be frustrating for parents and educators.

The more parents and educators attempt to push the teenager in the area in which they are gifted but not interested, the more the child will move away from it. We cannot force anyone to be passionate about anything, not even in an area where they have great gifts. As disheartening and disappointing as this may be, it is a reality we must accept. We can create situations that will attempt to nurture or create an interest, but it cannot be forced. We can hope that as time progresses they develop an interest in the field in which they are gifted, but we cannot make that happen.

If we determine that our students or children are passionate about something, we should do all we can to encourage them. We must never underestimate what passion and determination can produce. Passion can drive them to become very good at things in which they are not naturally gifted. It can often go further than natural giftedness. We often see this in athletics. The natural athlete will excel and be the star for years. However, the not-so-talented athlete, who has a real passion for the game and works constantly at developing his or her skills, will make the pros. We look at the example of Daniel "Rudy" Ruettiger. His story is so powerful that they created a movie entitled *Rudy* describing his determined effort to realize his dream. He was one of fourteen children and worked in the oil refinery. He dreamed of playing football for Notre Dame but had to overcome many obstacles to turn his dream into a reality.

He worked tirelessly at his academics, faced admittance rejections, had very little support, and slept in the maintenance room, until finally he was admitted to Notre Dame and made the football team as a walk-on player. He attended every practice even though he was not being played. Finally, in the last game of his senior year, the crowd began to chant, "Rudy, Rudy, Rudy." The coach played him for the last twenty-seven seconds of that game. While on the field, he sacked the quarterback and the crowd went crazy.

May we hope that our young people realize their dreams even when they are not gifted in that area. We can support and nurture their passions even when everything inside us tells us this child should be pursuing the area of his or her gifts.

One of the greatest gifts in life is to be passionate in, or about, something. Boredom, idle minds, lack of motivation, and a disinterest in the world are all poisonous. Having no interest in anything leads to apathy and depression. Having a passion about something is energizing, life-giving, and critical to living a fulfilling life.

Some teens pursue an area of life because they have been pushed into it. They may become doctors or lawyers since this profession will afford them a comfortable life, status, and prestige. However, they may never find happiness. They may satisfy their parents or fulfill worldly standards of success but never find peace. In addition to cheating themselves, they may have cheated the world of great contributions that could have been made in the area of their true passion.

We are not recommending that our teens be foolish. However, we do recommend that they dream and work at making their dreams come true. We do not want them to pursue a life passion that will result in poverty, but we do not want them to pursue a life that leaves them impoverished in the midst of their wealth.

Teenagers have to deal with many frustrations, changes, and stresses in their life. Pushing them to excel in an area that does not interest them will only lead to further stress and anxiety—even when they are good at it! Many teens have shared this frustration with us. Their parents recognize their talent and have pushed them into a career that will provide a very lucrative and comfortable life. The only problem is that the kids are not interested, and the pressure put on them causes great anxiety.

I remember teaching an attractive, talented, and intelligent student in a twelfth-grade religion class. Her father was a recognized and respected professional in the community. She could have done just about anything in life because of her academic abilities and wonderful personality. However, her one and true passion was dancing.

She explained to me her tremendous love and respect for her parents, her desire to make them happy and to live up to their expectations. Her parents, especially her father, saw no value or advantage to a life of dance, and disapproved of dance as a career.

As a result she passed up an opportunity to go to a renowned dance college in the United States. Because of her inability to pursue this as a career, she explained, she would never be completely happy. I felt sorry for her and often wondered how this may have affected her life.

Let's encourage our teenagers' pursuits in life, even when they do not appear to be lucrative or even practical. Their passions may become their hobbies later in life, as they pursue areas that provide a comfortable living. Now, we will have accomplished the best of both worlds.

A worker in one of the orphanages in Haiti said, "I have met many people from the Americas. They have said many things to me that I do not understand. Perhaps the most puzzling thing I have ever heard them say is, 'Time is money.' Can you imagine thinking this way when all the money in the world cannot buy one second of time!"

This Haitian taught me to live out every moment of my life more concerned about my passion than my possessions.

As difficult as it is to accept, we must resolve that there is something more important than status and financial comfort; it is responding to the passion that resides within us. Discovering and developing this passion will bring peace, happiness, and joy. If we are patient and we provide our children or students with the opportunity to discover and foster their passions, we will be surprised and satisfied with the outcome.

Dear God:
We know that you have gifted each of our children.
Help us to assist them in discovering the gifts
with which they have been blessed.
May we keep an open mind and be willing to introduce them
to many different interests in order to assist them
to realize their potential and their passion.
Help us to focus on our children
and not direct them or steer them
toward fulfilling our own dreams for them.
Keep us open to allowing them to live *their* dream.
We trust always in you, God,
knowing that with your grace we can accomplish this task.
Amen.

PRACTICAL TIPS

- Do not project your own dreams onto your child—
  empower your child to fulfill his or her own dreams.
- Determine your children's or students' gifts. Determine your
  children's or students' passion.
- Treasure passions. They are a gift; a fuel to dedication,
  which often surpasses natural giftedness.

POINTS TO PONDER

- What are your own dreams for your children or students?
  Are you putting pressure on your child to embrace certain
  dreams? For example, think of things you say or do regarding occupations.
- What are your children's or students' dreams?
- What does society say about your child's or student's
  dream?
- What do you think about your child's or student's dream?
- What can you do to help them realize their dreams?

SPIRITUAL EXERCISES

EXERCISE ONE

1. Read the following reflection written by Marianne Williamson:

   "Our deepest fear is not that we are inadequate. Our deepest fear is that we are powerful beyond measure. It is our light, not our darkness, that most frightens us. We ask ourselves, Who am I to be brilliant, gorgeous, talented, fabulous? Actually, who are you *not* to be? You are a child of God. Your playing small doesn't serve the world....We were born to make manifest the glory of God that is within us. It's not just in some of us it's in everyone. And as we let our own light shine, we unconsciously give other people permission to do the same. As we are liberated from our own fear, our presence automatically liberates others." Marianne Williamson, *A Return to Love: Reflections on the Principles of a Course in Miracles* (New York: Harper Collins, 1992), 190–91.

2. Have your children or students write or discuss their opinion on Marianne Williamson's reflection. Do they agree with what she is saying? How can we attempt to live out the greatness that is within us? What prevents us from living this out?

EXERCISE TWO

1. Read Matthew 25:14–29 (a gospel parable about using talents).
2. Ask your children or students to list the top five dreams they would like to pursue.
3. Ask them to write about the obstacles they face in reaching their dreams.
4. Ask them to discuss how they will overcome these obstacles in order to fulfill their dreams.
5. Conclude with Matthew 5:13–16 (salt of the earth/light of the world).

Chapter Eight

GUIDE THEM TO MODELS AND MENTORS

Clothe yourselves with the new self, created according to the likeness of God in true righteousness and holiness. (Eph 4:24)

All teenagers need role models and mentors. Many parents serve as excellent role models for their children. There is nothing more a child wants than to be proud of his father or mother and be just like them. The desire to model a parent is almost instinctual. For this reason, we as parents must make every effort to be outstanding people. In the life we live, the career we choose, the words we speak, the thoughts we think, the lessons we teach: we are to be our very best. This is the greatest challenge that we will face in life. We must exercise love, patience, prudence, and wisdom throughout every aspect of our life. When we do, our children will see our greatness and want to model this.

From a very young age, we desire to have someone we can look to as an inspiration and model. Many young people will refrain from deviant behavior just because they love and respect their parents so much that they do not want to disappoint them. Some kids will ask themselves before they decide to do something, "What will my parents think?" Some admit to thinking, "What would God think?" They ask themselves this not out of fear but rather out of love and respect.

However, not all teens have parents who can serve or should serve as their role models. If you fall into this category, it is never too late to make the necessary changes. Remember, your children want you to mentor them. Do not be afraid to recognize your own weakness and remember that our children do not expect us to be perfect.

There are also cases where parents are excellent role models. However, for one reason or another, their teenager has not chosen them as their hero to emulate. It could be that society's view of a hero is much different than the one established at home. It could be the powerful influence that friends have upon them. In this case, it is still important to be willing to serve as model and mentor, for at any time they may turn to you for this leadership. There are times however, when our youth turn to inappropriate and unhealthy role models. They can find themselves in gangs with gang leaders as their heroes. A gang will not judge their behavior in the traditional ways of the world. They will not reprimand them for deviant behavior or behavior that does not fit the traditional societal definition.

Many teens find comfort in this gang world. What the teenager cannot see is that these "mentors" will feed off their vulnerability and fears in order to satisfy themselves. Further, gang members and leaders live a fairly comfortable, exciting, adventurous, and almost romantic lifestyle. For the young teenager who does not trust society and has no role model, this gang life is attainable, romantic, and appealing. The initial desire to aspire to a good and productive life has died and has been replaced by the desire to become like the local drug dealer who drives a fancy car, is feared by others, has power, and has lots of money. Kids will be attracted to the gang leader who, he believes, will never mislead him, will always be loyal to him, and will always be honest with him. For the teenager disillusioned by society, this offer is appealing. These are qualities that this teenager has found difficult to find in society.

Although the majority of teenagers are not turning to gangs for direction, some turn to other places that may not be healthy. When working with teenagers we have to get them to return to "innocent" aspirations and see the rich reward in living a pure life with hard work and dedication. To do this, we need to expose our youth to people who have strong values and a diligent work ethic. Once a teenager has been exposed to these people—whether a popular athlete, a service worker, or a missionary—they will aspire to be like them. Teenagers love heroes and need models to follow. We all do.

One of the places our youth often turn to is the classroom. Educators can be excellent role models. The classroom teacher, for example, does more than impart knowledge. The Internet or library can provide that service. A teacher can be a student's hero. When a student connects with a teacher, success generally follows.

As educators we must be genuine, truly caring, empathetic, and always concerned for the well-being of our students. This is more important than marks. Students will respect and aspire to emulate the teacher who relates to them, is concerned about them, and will go out of their way to help them. For many of these kids, teachers become their parents away from home as well as their mentors and heroes.

We have witnessed many students who come back to visit their teachers. They come to visit, to say hello, and to catch up on what is new. They also come for another reason. They want to express their gratitude and appreciation for the love, inspiration, and guidance that teacher provided. They come to say thank you. These teachers are often invited to their weddings, their homes for dinner, and their children's baptism.

To our teenagers, a great teacher is first and foremost a person who has a great capacity to love. A great teacher is one who makes the student feel good about who they are and believes that they have something significant to offer the world. Good teachers elevate their students, making them feel important and valuable.

There are other opportunities to connect our children or students with heroes. We can connect them with other teenagers who exercise influence by their popularity and good character. For students who are struggling, we can connect them with people who have had similar experiences who have made some poor choices and suffered some severe consequences. Struggling students will listen to these people. When a person has experienced difficult times and is willing to share those times, students listen eagerly and intently.

We remember John, an individual that we both asked to visit our school and speak with the students on his life and some of the choices he made. John has cerebral palsy and is confined to a wheelchair. He speaks openly about what it was like for him growing up and being in high school. He recalls that instead of riding a Harley Davidson motorcycle, which was his dream, he rode his wheelchair. He willingly speaks about other difficult experiences: dating, friendships, and personal care.

In his talk, one of his most powerful stories is about his attempt to end his life. He recounts, with great emotion, his attempt to drive his wheelchair off a cliff. As he was in the midst of taking it over the cliff, he changed his mind. He redirected his chair with his electronic control and his chair fell over. Fortunately, he did not go over the cliff.

The students listen to John intently and respectfully. He shared with them his decisions and then reflected upon why those decisions were not good decisions. He recognized his errors and admits his mistakes. It does not mean that life for John has become easy. It will never be easy. However, he demonstrated to the kids how he has found peace and happiness in his chair. For some teenagers, John became a mentor and hero in the school. He was honest, forthright, and humble. He was willing to admit to his mistakes and most of all, in spite of his suffering, he ultimately chose to make the best of his life.

It is important that teenagers have role models and mentors. We can play a large role in directing them to people who can guide and direct them in making healthy choices. We need to explore opportunities that are available to us. Search within the community for people who would be a good mentor to your child. Most importantly, we as parents and educators must ourselves be living the life that is worthy of being a teenager's model and mentor.

> Dear God:
> We ask for the guidance of the Holy Spirit
> that we may be directed to a person or people
> who will serve as a good role model and mentor for [*child's name*].
> May we remain creative and open in our search.
> May we be lead in a direction that helps [*child's name*] to make good and healthy choices.
> May our words, actions, and lifestyle be worthy of offering direction
> and may [*child's name*] find renewed energy and direction as (*he/she*) makes decisions.
> Amen.

PRACTICAL TIPS

- Develop the image that we are all created in God's image, and it will provide a great model for your children or students.
- Investigate and become familiar with the various people who are at the schools, arenas, recreation centers, or other facilities that your children attend. Connect your children with those people in these facilities that are excellent role models.

· Invite people who are deserving of our respect and admiration into your classrooms and homes to share their stories.

POINTS TO PONDER

· What are you doing to contribute to the choosing and promoting of healthy role models in our schools and in our communities?
· Who are you defining as our heroes?
· What are your yardsticks for success? What does society use to measure success?

SPIRITUAL EXERCISES

EXERCISE ONE

Ask your children or students to select a person (living or dead) who is their greatest hero. Ask them to provide details about why they have chosen this person. What makes this person a hero to them?

EXERCISE TWO

1. Review the Beatitudes found in Matthew 5:1–12.
2. Ask your children or students to write about a person in their life who best lives the Beatitudes. Ask them to give specific examples of how the person lives each Beatitude. Finally, ask them to comment on how this person has impacted their life.

Chapter Nine

LOVE AND RESPECT THEM UNCONDITIONALLY

> I therefore, the prisoner in the Lord, beg you to lead a life worthy of the calling to which you have been called, with all humility and gentleness, with patience, bearing with one another in love.　　　　　　　　　　　　(Eph 4:1–2)

When you enter the home of a poor person in the mountains of the Dominican Republic, you are immediately greeted with love and respect. They don't know who you are, what your status is, or what you have accomplished. They love and respect you because of your humanity. They have no food and spend all day working hard to survive. They are consumed by crippling poverty. Yet, they treat you like royalty. They find food to cook for you, and they insist you eat. You are always served the food before they eat.

You are given a place of honor at their table. They expend great energy to entertain and converse with you, concerned about your happiness at that moment. When you leave, they often look for a gift to give you. After you leave, you feel sad because you miss them and the experience of unconditional love and respect they gave you.

In our world, youth are generally not offered unconditional respect and love. They are often not trusted and instead are held suspect for wrongdoing. We have often heard adults say that kids have to "earn" respect. Respect is not something that has to be earned. Our very being warrants respect. It is granted upon our birth. Respect can only be lost; however, it need not be earned.

Love is the other important component. This is probably the most important element in working with teens. We must love as Jesus asks of us: "Love as I have loved you" (John 13:34). We all make claim to loving our children and our students. However, love has different meanings for different people. We should always refer back to the love and respect Jesus exemplified. If we love unconditionally, in humility and with divine mercy, it will bring out the best in our teenagers.

Love and respect are the soil necessary to make healthy growth possible. Love and respect will foster confidence, security, conviction, and courage. Very often, we view respect in a hierarchical form. The more you succeed, in accord with society's view of success, the more respect you will receive. We live in a world where respect is mostly given to those who have power, money, or fame. Ideally, respect should be given to each person at birth by nature of their humanity. This respect should continue throughout a person's lifetime, from infancy to adulthood.

Women endured great suffering through the ages because they were denied the respect they deserved. Children were forced to endure horrible jobs and great hardships because they also received less respect. Those who were deformed, physically handicapped, or mentally ill were given little respect and often locked away from public view.

Think of how different the world would be if everyone were treated with respect. If we do not grant respect to all people, even the outcasts, we have missed the message of Jesus and instead create a world that is broken and divisive. Jesus reminds us repeatedly that it is in these very people that find him and, in turn, find the divine—in the weak, in the suffering, and in those who are in most need. Remember the words of Jesus in Matthew 25:40: "Just as you did it to one of the least of these…you did it to me."

Ironically, it is in these people that we often discover the greatest aspects of our humanity. When we see a homeless person on a park bench, we often make judgments about such people. Let us think for a minute, as our teenagers often do, of the suffering and the life experiences this person may have endured to get to that bench.

Remember Jesus' words when he spoke to St. Paul in his conversion:

"Saul, Saul, why do you persecute me?"
"Who are you, Lord?" Saul asked.
"I am Jesus, whom you are persecuting." (Acts 9:4–5)

When you persecute the least of his brothers and sisters, you persecute Jesus. All our prejudices, prejudgments, and opinions must be annihilated, and we must be forged together by our humanness as brothers and sisters. When we cannot strip ourselves naked to become one with all of humanity, granting infinite respect to all, we have broken away from our true nature and have lost our true freedom.

It is often the children with whom we have worked who demonstrate to us the importance of not judging, of forgiving and embracing humanity so that all people can be the best they can be.

It could be a fast-food restaurant, coffee shop, grocery store, or retail mall. Wherever you go, you can see teenagers working hard. For the most part, it is not adults performing these jobs but teenagers, who are willing to work hard for minimum wage, and they often do it with a smile. Teenagers, by the thousands, donate time to service groups and charities; they also work in the Third World.

How is it, then, that we are able to think negatively about our teenagers? Most are hard working and ambitious and approach life with joy. Teenagers take on these jobs in addition to their schoolwork, household chores, and extracurricular activities. This kind of work ethic and ambition is deserving of our ultimate respect. We cannot let a few who misbehave poison our attitude toward all teens. If we have a teenager who is in school and not doing well, we need not take away the love and respect that we have given to that young person. We need to determine why they are not doing well. What experiences or lessons have they been taught to cause this behavior? What kind of attitude did we impart to them and tolerate from them? Are they depressed? Do they suffer from a biochemical problem? There are so many questions to ask, and qualified doctors and therapists can help.

Good educators will acknowledge that every student in their school or class has potential. A great educator is one who says, "No matter what group or class I am working with, I know that there is a student who is more talented than I am and holds great potential to make a real difference in the world." This humble approach by educators and parents will facilitate heightened levels of respect toward all teenagers and ultimately lead to their flourishing.

While in the mountains of the Dominican Republic, I spent some time with a large, poor family. It was an extended family of roughly fifteen people, including aunts and uncles. They all lived in a one-room house of blocks. They knew that I was exploring poor areas to return home to raise money for these people.

They could have asked me to raise money for another house, food, clothing, medical supplies, chickens, goats, or a cow. Instead, they pleaded with me to raise money to build a school for them and their children. They chose a school over their most basic needs.

One of the daughters, aged sixteen or seventeen, was quiet and only listened. She was stunningly beautiful. Just as I was about to leave she told me, "Sir, if you raise the money and Father Lou builds a school, I promise never to get married and I will dedicate my life to becoming a teacher to teach my younger sisters and all the children of the village."

I was impressed, inspired, and shaken. Then I thought, "What lucky man will miss out in life if he cannot marry this beautiful girl?"

I responded, "We will raise the money and build you that school. But remember, sometimes teachers who are married make better teachers." She smiled as I left. Thanks to the generosity of the people back home we raised twenty thousand dollars to build that school.

By loving and respecting teenagers infinitely and unconditionally, we will teach them that respect is not about "doing"; it is about "being." We will teach them that respect is not about status, position, wealth, or power. Respect is about our humanness and humanity. We will show them that although we are there to nurture and guide them, we are also recipients waiting to be invited into their life so that we may receive and be nurtured by them. If we can do this, we will find ourselves entering a world filled with wisdom, innocence, adventure, and joy. That is the world of our teenagers.

You may recall the popular saying: *"Don't worry about yesterday. It's history. Don't worry about tomorrow. It's a mystery. Just enjoy today, which is a gift from God. That's why they call it the present."*

Too much thought analyzing yesterday and planning tomorrow takes away from the spontaneity of today. When we look at our children, we can see how yesterday and tomorrow do not consume them. This is one of the reasons why they are so spontaneous and why they know how to love life so much.

As we get older, our strong opinions, judgments, and traditions may imprison us. High expectations put on us by society and ourselves only cause us to be more guilt ridden, bitter, and cynical. Our children can teach us to be free of these kinds of preset prejudices. They can teach us that we are all lovable just because "we are." They challenge us to respect all people regardless of skin color, ethnicity, popularity, or accomplishments.

The high standards we set for our children serve only to compartmentalize them into becoming what *we* are, what *we* wish them to be, or what *we* wish *we* could have become. It has more to do with *us* than them. We have to put an end to our prejudices and judgments of the world and then we can end the prejudices of our teenagers. We have to give them and the world the respect and love they inherently receive at birth, not the respect and love they have to work endlessly trying to win. Most importantly, we have to stop making them victims of our own failures and misgivings. We cannot be afraid to be taught by them and even turn to them for help and support.

The greatest pearl in all of this is that they will lead and inspire us. Ironically, we will discover that when we fail and fall down, they will not judge us. Rather, they will be there to pick us up. Remember, deep down inside, we still remain their heroes and even heroes need help because even a just man will fall seven times a day.

St. Paul put it so beautifully: "As God's chosen ones, holy and beloved, clothe yourselves with compassion, kindness, humility, meekness, and patience. Bear with one another and, if anyone has a complaint against another, forgive each other; just as the Lord has forgiven you, so you also must forgive. Above all, clothe yourselves with love, which binds everything together in perfect harmony" (Col 3:12–14).

A beautiful story of kids in the Dominican Republic, and the kind of respect and love they show each other, is a helpful way to end this chapter.

One of the Canadian students who traveled to the Dominican Republic had a new Batman T-shirt that he had brought to give the poor. He had befriended a young Dominican child and gave the shirt to him. The child received the shirt with great happiness.

The next day, the student realized that another Dominican child had the Batman T-shirt on. It was a friend of the boy he had given it to. He said nothing.

The following day the student saw yet another Dominican child wearing the same Batman T-shirt. Again, he said nothing.

The next day there was again a different boy with the same shirt on. The student realized that no matter how great the gift, no matter how wonderful the pleasure of receiving it, the Dominican people received their greatest joy in sharing.

If we can give our teenagers the love and respect they deserve, they will each act accordingly to that love and respect. Most importantly, they will inspire us and introduce us to the innocent and joyful world we may have left behind when we left our own youth.

Dear God:
Help each of us to see your image in each of our children.
May we treat them with the love and respect they deserve.
May all children be granted the dignity, respect, and love
    that you, Lord, wish for them.
May we be your instruments to bring this to them.
Amen.

PRACTICAL TIPS

- Give children our respect and love. They deserve it.
- Offer love and respect to promote dignity and provide strength.
- Give children unconditional love, and the divine within them will be revealed.

POINTS TO PONDER

- Do you love your children/students unconditionally?
- Do you believe our youth are deserving of our respect?
- What can we do to highlight some of the great accomplishments of our youth?

SPIRITUAL EXERCISES

1. Place a number of stones in a burlap sack. Take the sack and ask the children or students to take one stone and pass the sack around. Ask them to hold the stone in their hands. Then read John 8:1–11.
2. Discuss with them Jesus' response. Comment on the fact that, unlike the people who brought the woman to Jesus, he was not interested in the gossip or the sin.

3. Ask the children or students to think about an act for which they wish to have forgiveness—an act they are not proud of, or an act they wish did not happen.
4. Pass around a sack and have each child or student place the stone back in the sack.
5. Remind them of the unconditional love Jesus has for them and the mercy he offers. Read the words Jesus said at the time of his crucifixion: "Father, forgive them, for they do not know what they are doing" (Luke 23:34).
6. Remind them that Jesus asks us to be filled with mercy and forgiveness. How many times does Jesus ask us to forgive? Then read Matthew 18:21–35.

Chapter Ten

GIVE THEM ENOUGH AUTONOMY TO HAVE CONFIDENCE

> Let us therefore no longer pass judgment on one another, but resolve instead never to put a stumbling block or hindrance in the way of another....Let us then pursue what makes for peace and for mutual upbuilding. (Rom 14:13, 19)

When teenagers leave home for college, those who were under a strict rule at home with no autonomy usually end up celebrating a little too much. Those who were given too much freedom, absent of any rules or regulations, often continue to party in the same spirit. Those who lived with rules and freedoms that were established in a democratic homelife, where the teen was given autonomy, are the students who are likely to find the proper balance. They exercise the greatest amount of discipline and are able to excel in college.

Thankfully, many of us are reluctant to give our teenagers too much freedom. We fear that they may abuse the freedom, lose a sense of responsibility associated with the freedom, and run wild with their instincts and wants, devoid of any rational thought. When too much freedom is given to any of us, this can occur. Even as adults, we need structure and parameters. Very few of us can handle total freedom. We need to be guided by employers who are good leaders, to be reminded of our responsibilities at home, and to be regulated in daily life by government laws. Without these guides, our lives become confused, chaotic, and destructive. Very few of us are completely self-motivated, self-regulated, and self-disciplined.

Teenagers are no different. They cannot handle total freedom. Not only will it bring chaos and destruction to their lives, it gives them the impression that their family, school, and church do not really care about their well-being. Therefore, teenagers need rules, regulations, restrictions, and expectations set for them. The rules must be created because we care for them, love them, and want to protect them. We also want to work toward preserving the common good. Fair rules, created in a democratic way, are signs of love and concern.

The difference between the adult world and the teen world is that in the adult world we are given a voice in establishing our rules and restrictions. At work, we have unions that speak on our behalf to maintain our justified freedoms. On a government level, we have the freedom to vote and choose those who will represent us and be attentive to our opinions and philosophy. In the judicial system, we have the right to sue or challenge injustices or restrictions imposed upon us that we deem unjust. In many situations, we have arbitrators at our disposal. On a personal level, we usually have an equal partnership with our spouses in establishing the expectations and responsibilities of family life. Teenagers do not enjoy any of these privileges. In this way, they are often limited in their autonomy.

When we look at any empire or kingdom in history, we observe that eventual revolution and fall occurred when people were deprived of their autonomy and denied their voice. Teenagers find themselves as recipients of rules, regulations, restrictions, and expectations imposed upon them. They have little or no voice in government, school, society, or home. They cannot solicit a powerful union and in most cases will not retain a lawyer or arbitrator to act on their behalf. Politicians pay little or no attention to the voice of kids, perhaps because they do not vote and, of those who can, have a low turnout rate. Still very dependent on family and society for financial and personal needs, they allow themselves to be subjects without rebellion.

Some teenagers, however, have been under such strong authority that they take the risk and strike back. This may happen more often with teenagers who have experienced abusive authority at home. Authority expressed in a home through yelling, name-calling, put-downs, and constant criticism will harden a child. When authority does not allow them to voice their opinions or have any say in life, a teenager's response can become explosive. They become fearless of the consequences from family or society. Fueled by anger and frustration, they will rebel, and in so doing, they often choose a road to disaster. Lacking the knowledge and wisdom to make the right choices, and being motivated by anger, they are often destined for disaster.

81

We must change our views. Many youth, now at the age of reason, are gifted with tremendous wisdom and have every right to help shape and direct their own lives. We have to give them some freedom to participate in establishing their rules, regulations, and responsibilities. This democratic approach gives them their autonomy, control, and authority over their own lives. The home, school, and society should grant the kids a voice just as they do with adults. When we hand over this kind of autonomy to our children, we will create in them a stronger sense of self, a more mature approach to life, and a more responsible and wholesome development.

We are well aware of the importance in the balance between laws and freedoms; however, with teenagers we tend to forget this. They should play a democratic role in establishing these rules and freedoms. They have to play this important and responsible role in their home, school, and community.

An eighteen-year-old teenager once said: "I can drive a car, which is the most lethal weapon in our society. I am expected to score honor marks in school, hold down a job to support my own expenses and school fees, could be drafted and give my life for my country, but I can't have a beer until I am nineteen and have no say in how anything runs." There certainly are many contradictions in our society and our teenagers see it.

When we give our teenagers more autonomy in directing their life, in making decisions that shape their world, we will create a stronger and healthier teenage generation. A sense of autonomy involves more than shaping the external world of the teenager. It has a powerful effect on molding the interior of the individual. This sense of autonomy brings with it a sense of identity, importance, and most of all, dignity.

When parenting and working with teenagers, much of what we should do is listen to them as they discover the answers. Encourage them to lead. Challenge them to take freedoms and responsibilities and to shape their life. Expect them to create the rules that will regulate their own life. When they know that their opinions, values, and judgments are respected, they develop a strong sense of responsibility, and with this freedom, we can work together in a democratic way to arrive at what is wholesome.

Once we give them this autonomy, they gain confidence in themselves and what they have to offer. They will be more responsible and productive contributors, rather than just recipients. Building this sense of confidence and responsibility through granting them autonomy is critical. It is a frustrating experience to meet a teenager who has tremendous talent and ability but lacks confidence. All teenagers have gifts, and gaining confidence helps their gifts flourish.

The school was preparing for its annual "think fast" in which students fast for thirty-five hours and spend the night at the school. This is an overnight event that generally commands a large crowd. It is so successful that the number of participants is limited ahead of time. Students were admitted on a first-come, first-served basis. They love this event and look forward to it. The money that they raise assists the poor in developing countries.

It was a great deal of work and I would always get the assistance of the students. They would help with the planning of activities and overall organization of events that take place over the thirty-five hours.

One year I had a student tell me that he would be willing to take it over for me. He would organize the entire event. I thought for a moment and then agreed.

When he left, I began to worry and ask myself, "How could he accomplish all that needed to be done? How could he set the rules, make the decisions, and organize the entire event?" I was sure that this was beyond his or any other student's ability. I could hardly handle the task myself as an adult!

This student proved me wrong. He organized the entire event and it went off without a glitch. The students said the event was the best ever. The activities were great, the rules were reasonable, and the atmosphere was enjoyable. I was amazed.

This experience revealed to me that I doubted when I shouldn't have. I was reluctant to give this student and his team the flexibility and power to make their own decisions and run the event. The student, however, knew when he needed my input and he would come to me before making decisions. I gave him autonomy, and this gave him confidence. The results were awesome!

Every teenager and adult deserves and needs confidence. We all need to be confident in ourselves and in our abilities. We require the courage to take risks in life, to try new adventures, to explore different avenues, and to do it with pride and confidence. Confidence and courage are major ingredients for success. Part of that courage and confidence will be imparted when we give our teenagers the freedom and autonomy to begin shaping their world prior to adulthood.

You can have two teenagers with the same level of intelligence, but it's the student with confidence who will excel. The student given autonomy over one's life and who has played an active role in shaping their life will be the successful one.

Once you breathe courage and confidence into children and students by supporting their gifts and giving them autonomy, they will succeed. We can then progress to more difficult challenges that facilitate more freedom and autonomy. Even if we have to step in behind the scenes, we do that to ensure they succeed. As their confidence develops, they will become more independent and bold. It is a good time to remind them that a person is never a failure unless they quit.

Building confidence and imparting autonomy is critical to empowering young people to develop to their full potential. The difference in their ability is staggering once they know that their opinion will be valued and used to shape their world.

Dear God:
Let us view our teenagers as powerful
    and worthwhile beyond measure.
Enable us to see the great contributions
    that they can make to make this world a better place.
Assist us in learning about them,
    intimately and carefully so that we can provide them
    with the autonomy and confidence in themselves
    that enable them to excel.
Amen.

PRACTICAL TIPS

- Remember that our youth are wise and often are able to see through things that clutter the adult mind.
- Include youth in formulating the rules that govern their lives.
- Make youth a part of the decision-making process, and they will more readily take ownership and be more willing to accept consequences.

POINTS TO PONDER

- When is the last time your children or students gave input into setting rules, curfews, or expectations?
- Do you value and respect the input of our youth? Do you listen and take their comments and suggestions into consideration?
- How do you feel when you are subjected to a decision where you were not consulted? How do you feel when you were consulted and your comments were clearly dismissed?

SPIRITUAL EXERCISES

EXERCISE ONE

1. Tell your students that for this exercise they will be responsible for creating and running their own school.
2. Ask them, as a class, to establish the rules and guidelines most important to insuring the school is run fairly and well. (They are to do this on their own. You, as teacher, are simply there to observe.)
3. Ask them to rank and list the five most important rules and guidelines.
4. At the end of the exercise, you enter the discussion. Discuss with them which of the items could be implemented in the classroom for the next week. Come to agreement with them (insure you are listening and accepting their input). Insure that the plan includes consequences and punishments for violations.
5. When the week is over, discuss the experience. How did it work out? Did they feel it was fair? Were they able to abide by it?

EXERCISE TWO

This is an exercise that can be used as an icebreaker and confidence-builder. It is meant to make students feel comfortable in the classroom. Comfort builds confidence.

1. All participants form a circle.
2. The first person begins by stating their name.
3. The next person in the circle repeats the first person's name and adds their name. For example, "That's Katie and I am Patrick." You may also ask your students to clap and keep a beat during the responses. Each person must say the names of all those who have gone before them. You complete this for the entire circle. If a student cannot remember a name, the person whose name they forget may help.
4. You then begin again and this time each person adds one word that describes a trait about him or herself. The word they use must begin with the same letter of their first name. For example: Sweet Susan or Jack the Joker. The circle continues in the same format where the person that follows must repeat all previous speakers' responses.
5. Once you finish, you add one more rotation. This time each person repeats their name, their trait, and adds an action or gesture—which can mean anything as simple as making a peace sign, making a funny facial expression, making a handshake gesture, or spontaneously using the objects at hand as props. Some students are more expressive with dance steps, or more. The next person once again repeats all previous speakers' responses and gestures and then adds their own gesture.

The First two rounds are very funny and work much better than the traditional icebreaker. The third round is of course the funniest and makes a class into a real "group."

Conclusion

LIGHT AND HOPE

"I can do all things through him [Christ] who strengthens me."
(Phil 4:13)

You are on this journey with your children or your students because God has called you. You have taken the time to read and work through the formula presented here because you care. You know that Jesus is with you every step of the way. As a result, you must be filled with hope and confidence.

Suffering and joy are merely two sides of the same coin, intimately connected in a mysterious and spiritual way. As we suffer in our struggle and desire to elevate our students and children, we know that it is as a result of our care, concern, and love for them. This is understandable, logical, and reasonable. We need to put this in perspective and never let it consume us, conquer us, or overpower us.

Jesus speaks directly to us when he says: "Come to me, all you that are weary and are carrying heavy burdens, and I will give you rest. Take my yoke upon you, and learn from me: for I am gentle and humble in heart, and you will find rest for your souls. For my yoke is easy, and my burden is light" (Matt 11:28–30).

God has called you and your children to be the light of the world. "You are the light of the world. A city built on a hill cannot be hid. No one after lighting a lamp puts it under a bushel basket, but on the lamp stand, and it gives light to all the house. In the same way, let your light shine before others, so that they may see your good works and give glory to your Father in heaven" (Matt 5:14–16). When we build up our children and students, we build up ourselves. We bring light to what is often a dark world. We must always work to let the light shine!

Upon leaving the mission in Mexico, the sisters pointed to the door of my room and said, "Peter, see that door? It is always open for you!"

The door is always open for our teens and inside is a place where teenagers can find their home, discover how great they are, and be given the opportunity to change the world.

We conclude our journey with this prayer (next page) written on the first anniversary of the martyrdom of Archbishop Oscar Romero (and often mistakenly attributed to him). As the prayer says, may we continue to recognize that we may not be able to do it all. However, there is greatness in what we *can* do, trying to bring out the greatness in our teenagers.

"Prophets of a Future Not Our Own"

A Reflection on the Martyrdom
of Archbishop Oscar Romero

It helps, now and then, to step back and take the long view.

The kingdom is not only beyond our efforts,
it is even beyond our vision.
We accomplish in our lifetime only a tiny fraction
of the magnificent enterprise that is God's work.
Nothing we do is complete, which is a way of saying
that the kingdom always lies beyond us.

No statement says all that could be said.
No prayer fully expresses our faith.
No confession brings perfection.
No pastoral visit brings wholeness.
No program accomplishes the church's mission.
No set of goals and objectives includes everything.

This is what we are about.
We plant the seeds that one day will grow.
We water seeds already planted, knowing that they hold future
    promise.
We lay foundations that will need further development.
We provide yeast that produces far beyond our capabilities.

We cannot do everything, and there is a sense of liberation in
    realizing that.
This enables us to do something, and to do it very well.
It may be incomplete, but it is a beginning, a step along the way,
an opportunity for the Lord's grace to enter and do the rest.
We may never see the end results, but that is the difference
between the master builder and the worker.

We are workers, not master builders; ministers, not messiahs.
We are prophets of a future not our own.

Ken Untener, Bishop of Saginaw, died 2004

May God bless you!